WHAT MY FATHER DIDN'T TEACH ME

LESSONS I HAD TO LEARN ON MY OWN

TERRENCE JAMESON

Inspired Word Publishers

Printed in the United States of America

ISBN-13: 978-0692124338

ISBN-10: 0692124330

To my beautiful and loving wife, my son, and my daughter.

You share my heart.

You are my inspiration.

Your welfare is what motivates me.

To my mother, thank you for giving me a chance at life.

TABLE OF CONTENTS

WHY I WROTE THIS BOOK

I could no longer avoid writing this book. I had to write this book. For ten years, I let other things take precedence over what may very well be my life's work. There are some stories that absolutely must be told and there are life experiences that must be shared. There was a burning desire within me to share what I have learned, things I wish I could have learned from my parents, particularly my father – if he was around.

Although my mother raised my younger brother and me, by herself, to the best of her ability, as I grew older, I found that she was unable to give me a much-needed male perspective, particularly as the challenges facing a young African-American male living in the United States became more complex.

I offer no excuse for the outcome of my life. Although my father has been absent throughout my life, this is not the story of a fatherless victim – someone that has suffered because of an absentee dad. No, this is the story of someone that has succeeded despite not having a father, or a father figure, during my formative years.

My purpose for writing this book is to share with you the many life principles that I have learned throughout my life; important principles that I wish I had learned much earlier, from my father. These are not ordinary principles. These are powerful, life-changing principles that, had I learned earlier in childhood or adolescence, the trajectory and pace of my life would have been much different. Indeed, I would have had a substantial head start in life. Isn't this what everyone wishes they had – a head start?

I cannot turn back the clock. I do not get a do-over or what they call a mulligan in golf. That's okay. However, what I can do is share with you precious principles that can help you – a young man or woman, a middle-aged adult, a senior citizen, or someone looking for sound advice – impact your life or the life of someone you know in a positive way. This is the fulfilling of my purpose, my gift to you, and my gift to the world.

WHY YOU SHOULD READ THIS BOOK

We all have to run this race – this thing called life. Life is a shared experience. We cannot experience it by ourselves. Life is a complex, challenging journey that can be quite difficult at times with winding roads, steep cliffs, and treacherous bends. Some people like to experience these obstacles by themselves without aid or help from others. For the wise journeyman, a little direction from someone who has previously traveled the terrain is usually appreciated, especially if it can help you to avoid common mistakes and silly pitfalls, some of which are very unforgiving and can dramatically alter your path and future success.

Do you ever wonder why some people are happier, more successful, and seem to have everything figured out?

Are they just lucky while everyone else was dealt a bad hand?

What if you discover the only difference between you and them is that you never learned the simple, yet incredibly powerful lessons needed to unlock your highest potential to enable you to experience the type of life you want for yourself?

This is my promise to you. No matter your gender, race, ethnicity, or age, this book contains something that you may not have considered or perhaps did not know before and need to learn in order to change the trajectory of your future. The target audience for this book is anyone that desires to lead a more fulfilling and abundant life; someone that wants to escape the matrix of mediocrity and live the life that others will, sadly, never achieve.

What My Father Didn't Teach Me: Lessons I Had to Learn On My Own is not just a book about the lessons I have learned. This is a book about sound life principles that, if followed, have the power to alter the course of your life in a positive way and the life of those around you – the people that are, or someday will be, most important to you. You are about to learn life lessons, important principles that are invaluable. You will forever be changed!

PART 1

A LIFE OF PURPOSE

We all have something amazingly special in us, and you solely owe it to yourself to discover yours. – Edmond Mbiaka

When you lose sight of your path, listen for the destination in your heart. – Katsura Hoshino

Your purpose in life is to find your purpose and give your whole heart and soul to it. – Gautama Buddha

1

PURSUE YOUR PASSIONS

People with passion can change the world for the better. – Steve Jobs

If you have a strong purpose in life, you don't have to be pushed. Your passion will drive you there. – Roy T. Bennett

It is not enough to be industrious; so are the ants. What are you industrious about? – Henry David Thoreau

There are three motives for which all humans live; we live for the body, we live for the mind, and we live for the soul. Regardless of what many may say, we can never truly be happy or satisfied if one of the three is neglected. All three are important.

Man cannot live fully in body if certain needs are not met. Without proper food and clean water, comfortable clothing, adequate shelter, and freedom from excessive work, life is extremely difficult and burdensome. Sufficient rest and recreation are essential to maintaining physical health and vitality of mind.

Man cannot live fully in mind without books and time to read them, without an opportunity to travel and observe, or without intellectual companionship or stimulus. To live fully in mind, one must have intellectual pursuits and must seek out opportunities to enjoy substances he is capable of using and enjoying. All work and no play makes Jack a dull boy.

To live fully in soul, man must have love. A man's highest happiness is found in the bestowal of benefits and looking after the welfare of those he loves. Love finds its most natural expression in giving. The Bible says that God so loved the world that He *gave*. To love is to give. The man who has nothing to give cannot fulfill his duty as a husband, father, citizen, or as a man. Therefore, it's essential for a man to have something to give whether it's his time, possessions, or life.

Love is denied expression if any of these three are withheld. It is the act of loving, through giving, that creates treasure in heaven.

To truly be happy, a life must include the development and advancement of the body, mind, and soul. Only then can we fulfill our purpose and maximize our fullest potential. The purpose of our creation is the advancement and unfoldment of life. Therefore, each man is given, in proportion to his ability, the tools to contribute to the refinement, beauty, and richness of life. To be content with less is sinful and will bring reproach. Not failure but low aim is sin.

Set Your Own Path

Your happiness is your personal responsibility.

It's no one's job to make you happy.

Who else can better understand how you think, what you feel, and what is important to you?

However, this will not stop some individuals from trying to determine what is good for you or what is in your best interest. If you let them, they will cunningly convince you that what is really in *their* best interest is yours. Said differently, they will try to make their agenda your agenda, and if you are not working to make your dreams possible, you are probably working to develop the dreams of someone else.

You may have to learn how to politely, yet forcefully, say "no." Sometimes, the following phrases must become part of your vocabulary: "No, I can't do that right now"; "No, I don't believe that is in my best interest"; and "If you feel so strongly about it why don't you do it yourself." You must learn to defend yourself. Few people are going to stick up for you if you do not stick up for yourself.

I recall a brief period in my life when I served as the Head Elder at the church I attended. After receiving my undergraduate degree, I left home to pursue work opportunities in various cities across the country. During this time, I also completed my graduate degree. After spending six years away, I moved back to Nebraska and resumed attending my home church. I served as an elder previously, but this time the pastor of the church was different. He was a young and powerful speaker, full of charisma having recently graduated from seminary, and accepted the call to pastor a small church located in a state he later admitted he had to look up on a map. We hit it off right away. We both had big aspirations and wanted to be successful in our professional career.

As a senior pastor with no pastoral staff for support, he needed considerable help from the local church elders to carry out his initiatives. He sized this group up quickly, taking stock of the hand he was dealt, and told me that he wanted me to be his Head Elder. Not fully understanding the responsibilities that I would be taking on, and the plans the pastor had for my life, I graciously accepted the position. The other elders, all senior to me in age, agreed.

I soon learned just how demanding the job would be. Although church leadership was not my full-time job, the Pastor found this hard to accept. His success, and the success of the church, required committed workers who would dedicate their time to his goal – turning a small inconspicuous church into one that is known throughout the Omaha community. Whereas the other elders were married with children, I was a bachelor with no family commitments. Therefore, the Pastor did not hold back in appointing duties that consumed my evenings and weekends. I had very little time for the things I deemed important, like dating or pursuing a professional certification to advance my career. I discussed this with the Pastor and was told what could be more important than the souls in Omaha needing to be saved, and perhaps maybe it's not God's will for me to have a wife. I soon realized if things continued this way, I would be living according to his agenda and not my own.

It's imperative that you charter your own course in life. Be responsible for *your* future and condition in life so if things do not go as expected you have no one to blame but yourself. If you fail at something – it will be *your* failure, but if you are successful – it will be *your* success. With the exception of your parents, your spouse, a few loyal friends, or a trusted mentor, no one else will be able to share the credit. Don't put yourself in a situation where one day you realize that you are unhappy because you followed someone else's advice. The only comfort they will be able to provide is a sincere, yet weak, apology – if they apologize at all.

Consider a teenage girl that succumbs to peer pressure and reluctantly decides to have sex with her adolescent boyfriend because "everyone is doing it." She, not her friends, ends up getting pregnant or worse, contracts a life-threatening disease. Either situation is undesirable, but it's compounded or made worse because not only must she live with the outcome, she has to live with the regret that her decision was heavily influenced by others.

After recognizing and accepting the responsibility for making your own decisions, pursue your passions feverishly for this will provide the greatest long-term rewards, happiness, and achievement.

GUARD YOUR TIME AND PURSUE YOUR PASSION

The lifespan of humans is very short. If we are lucky, we may live to see our eightieth birthday. Our natural progression in life is that we are born; we become toddlers, young children, then teenagers, and eventually young adults. Around the age of 18 is roughly the time when most people start to work...and we work, work, and work until we reach retirement at the age of 65. We spend the majority of our adult life, almost 50 years, working. This is why time is very important. You should spend the majority of your adult years, when you have more control of your time, doing something that you enjoy versus doing something that you dislike. Most people can look back upon their days of childhood with fondness. If you plan well, the years spent in retirement can also be enjoyable.

But what about the years in between?

Those years should not be wasted or written off because once those years are gone they are gone forever.

If you find yourself working in a job that you hate, just to receive a paycheck, then it's time for you to make a change in your life. It's time for you to stop settling. It's time for you to reinvent yourself. It's never too late to start. Life is just too short.

11

Make the most of each day you are given. Don't give yourself an occasion to experience regret by looking back over all the years that could have been used to pursue your passions.

Never make excuses for why you do not pursue your passions. A person that claims that they do not have access to the right resources is often making an excuse for why they are not doing more to advance their current situation. Instead of resources, what they lack is generally the right mindset; they have a defeatist mentality. Success begins by having the right mindset. Henry Ford once said, "If you think you can or if you think you can't, you're right."

Never say that you do not have access to the right things because that is often an automatic excuse. If you really want something bad enough, you will find a way to get it. Passion, when combined with talent, will make a way for itself, especially if it's something you truly want. This is why people should only pursue things they truly love. Because if you do not love it, and are not willing to persistently pursue it, you probably will not be successful anyway.

Sometimes, you have to do transitional jobs in order to get to where you want to go.

Don't allow your current situation or a temporary setback dictate your future.

It's okay if you do not get a full-ride athletic scholarship to attend a Division I school. Go to the Division II School, or junior college, that offered you a scholarship and get a free education. Numerous current and former professional athletes that attended little-known colleges went on to have successful careers playing professional sports.

Make the most of the opportunities available to you. Do your assigned job with pride. Solomon said,

> "Whatever you do, do well. For when you go to the grave, there will be no work or planning or knowledge or wisdom" (Ecclesiastes 9:10).

Abraham Lincoln said something similar when he said, "Whatever you are, be a good one."

Don't give up on your dreams. Don't let your current situation kill your dream because sometimes the only thing that makes life bearable is your dream. You have to keep saying, "I am going to do this. Failure is not an option." Not, "'I'm thinking about doing this' or, 'I want to do this'."

No! Your thoughts and words must be, "I am going to do this."

This is why you must be passionate about your pursuits. You have to love it. It must consume you. It must be one of the reasons why you exist. Once you have this mindset, then no matter what your goal is, whether it's writing a book, becoming a professional athlete, actor, doctor, lawyer, anything, if it's your passion, you are going to achieve it.

It doesn't matter how many times you fall down. Get back up. Keep moving forward. This is how you move from crawling to walking. You fall. Then, you get back up. You fall again, but you keep getting up. Eventually, you will learn how to keep your balance and are able to stand. Then, you will eventually learn how to put one foot in front of the other to begin walking. Once you are able to walk, you are now free to run. When you are able to run, you can begin pursuing better, more efficient ways of moving forward faster. You can learn to ride a bicycle. This will be another lesson of falling and getting back up. But it all started with having the courage and determination to get back up. Once you understand this, nothing can stop you.

What Is Passion?

Merriam-Webster dictionary defines passion as *an emotion, an intense, driving, or overmastering feeling or conviction; a strong liking or desire for a devotion to some activity.* However, passion is better defined by what it does and what it looks like.

Passion is a basketball player shooting 1,000 shots after practice is over and everyone else has left the gym. Passion is a schoolteacher continuing to work in an inner-city school with "those" kids instead of taking a job at a private or charter school. Passion is a scientist toiling away in a laboratory to discover hundreds of products using peanuts, sweet potatoes and soybeans. Passion is a medical doctor leaving home to render medical aid in a foreign country during a pandemic. Lastly, passion is our Creator not giving up on mankind and developing a plan for our redemption.

When you pursue your passions, work will not seem like work. Where others see failure, you see success. Where others say, "I won't" you respond with an affirmative "I will."

Passion is not motivated by money or financial reward.

I believe that everyone should be recognized or monetarily rewarded for their contributions, particularly if it uplifts society and the world in which we live, but a person whose motive is guided by passion remains committed even if the gain is minimal.

REDEFINE YOUR DEFINITION OF SUCCESS

Success is not easily defined. The definition is relative; it can mean different things for different people due to time, circumstances, and location among others. However, let's be honest. For most people in the world, money is success. The more money you have, the more successful you are.

This belief is wrong. Success is becoming what you want to be, achieving your objectives and goals, living a full life that satisfies your passions.

Be careful of letting someone dictate to you what success should look like. There are many miserable, insecure people that will never be satisfied and will always find a reason to criticize – ever seeking to assert their opinion on others.

I read a short story that summarized this best. The story goes like this:

One man, a CEO, decided to explain the problem with education. He argued, "What's a kid going to learn from someone who decided his best option in life was to become a teacher?" To stress his point, he said to another guest; "You're a teacher, Katherine. Be honest. What do you make?"

Teacher Katherine, who had a reputation for honesty and frankness replied, "You want to know what I make?" (She paused for a second then began...) "Well, I make kids work harder than they ever thought they could. I make a C+ feel like the Congressional Medal of Honor winner. I make kids sit through 40 minutes of class time when their parents can't make them sit for 5 minutes without an iPod, Gameboy, or movie rental. Do you really want to know what I make?"

(She paused again and looked at each and every person sitting at the table)

"I make kids wonder. I make them question. I make them apologize and mean it. I make them have respect and take responsibility for their action. I teach them how to write and then make them write. Keyboarding isn't everything. I make them read, read, read. I make them show all their work in math. They use their God-given brain, not a man-made calculator. I make my students from other countries learn everything they need to know about English...while preserving their unique cultural identity. I make my classroom a place where all my students feel safe and secure. Finally, I make them understand that if they use the gifts they were given, work hard, and follow their hearts – they can succeed in life."

(Katherine paused one last time and then continued)

"Then, when people try to judge me by what I make...I can hold my head up high and pay no attention because they are so ignorant. You want to know what I make? I make a difference in all your lives, educating your kids...and preparing them to become CEO's, and doctors, and engineers. What do you make Mr. CEO?" His jaw dropped and he went silent.

Nothing further needs to be said regarding letting someone's opinion of your achievement in life shape how you perceive yourself.

You don't have to be perfect in order to be good. For some, nothing is ever, or will ever be, good enough; they will never be satisfied. However, unless safety is an issue – for most things, the world does not demand or require perfection for acceptable results to be achieved. A score of 90% on an end of course exam is not perfect but is more than sufficient. A lifetime batting average of .340 over a 15-year career playing major league baseball is not perfect; it means that over 60% of the time you did not make it to first base, but it nonetheless places you in elite company – earning you a place in Cooperstown, New York at the National Baseball Hall of Fame.

Most things in life are not a matter of life and death. This does not mean that you should be comfortable with mediocrity. You should give your level best in each of your undertakings and endeavors. Be honest with yourself. Deep down inside, in a quiet moment of reflection, you know whether you gave your best effort.

Every community on earth, in order to ensure forward advancement, requires each citizen to contribute the maximum of his or her capabilities. Over time, as each individual strives to do their best, there will be steady improvement in the areas of life that raises living standards and the quality of life, such as healthcare, water and food quality, housing, education, and manufacturing.

Success has an element of competitiveness, but it does not have to be a zero-sum game – meaning for there to be a winner there must be a loser. In sports, there is only one winner, but life is not a game; someone does not have to lose in order for you to win. To better understand this truth, you may need to expand your understanding of success because things are not always as they seem.

As an example, let's consider several automobile manufacturers competing to sell cars. The company that gains the largest share of the market will sell the most cars and will appear on paper as the most successful. However, you have to look beyond the numbers by analyzing the whole business. You must understand the factors that enabled the company to obtain the largest percent of the market.

Here are a few questions that need to be answered. Was the company the first automobile manufacturer to enter the market? Is the company selling cars at too low a price, and if so, how long can it do this and still make a profit? Is their business strategy sustainable?

Market share is either growing or decreasing; it will not remain the same. A few years of robust sales does not create a legacy.

After close inspection, you learn the company was able to obtain the largest share of the market by selling attractively designed cars intended for middle-income wage earners, sold at a price much lower than its competitors. But in order to achieve the desired profit margin, the company had to find ways to cut costs. The company's management decided to pay nominal wages to its employees, reduce research and development expenditures, use cheap materials, and offer a limited repair warranty.

Let me ask you something.

Is this really winning?

Do the company's customers really benefit from purchasing these cars?

Does the comfort of having a job offset the psychological effects of working for a company that manufacturers and sales cheap cars?

The long-term benefits are few.

The short-term benefit of buying a car from this company is that you save money on the initial purchase. For the company's employees, the short-term benefit is obviously the paycheck and possibly much needed health insurance coverage.

In either case, whether a person is a customer or an employee, the primary motive for affiliating with the company is money – to save money or to make money. The company's purpose and the reason for existence are also very clear – to make money. However, the company's CEO will try to dress this up by saying the company's mission is to manufacture and provide affordable cars.

With this business strategy, it won't take long before the low-cost provider's share of the market begins to decline. By paying lower wages relative to its peers, employee morale will suffer and this will lead to inefficiency, which will lead to higher operating costs. The first customers to buy the vehicles will become a choir of critics, raising their complaints to anyone willing to hear about cheap parts that wear down easily, poor customer service – especially when the car needs servicing, and how the car's exterior cracked like an eggshell when involved in a minor accident. Because of the low price, the company may indeed retain a respectable share of the market even with the bad publicity.

Let me show you an alternative operating philosophy and definition of winning.

One of the company's competitors took a different approach by making quality cars and employee satisfaction their primary objective. Quality cars and employee satisfaction were embedded in the company's mission statement and part of the corporate culture. First, the company spent a lot of money on research and development with the purpose of building safe vehicles that would protect passengers during an accident. The company invested in quality materials. It offered a five-year warranty that covered all the major parts. The company paid its employees a higher wage and offered bonuses for achieving productivity and efficiency targets. The company provided tuition reimbursement to employees pursuing a college degree.

Operational costs were higher and this made the company's profit margin lower. The company's "quality and employees first" strategy came with the understanding that the company would have to make up the difference by selling more cars if it was to match the market leader in net income. The company's ownership and management team were different. They believed that net income is not the sole measure of success. The company's primary motive for operating was to sell safe, well-manufactured cars while raising the standard of living of employees by paying honorable wages and providing a desirable work environment. For this company, this is how it defined winning.

Profitability is important for any business if it is to be sustained, but the reason for *doing business* is more important.

CHAPTER SUMMARY

To have a full and happy life you must nurture your body, mind, and soul. To be truly happy, a life must include the development and advancement of each of these three. Only then can you be happy, fulfill your purpose, and maximize your fullest potential.

The advancement and fullest potential of society depend on each citizen giving their level best. By pursuing your passions, those things for which you care about and are most dedicated, the hard work that lies ahead will not seem like work because passion is not motivated by money.

When pursuing your passions, it's important that you define success and be careful not to let another person's opinion influence how you perceive yourself.

Prioritize who you are, and who you want to be. For you, success may mean having good health. Maybe it's having a happy marriage. Maybe it's living a single life while helping others. Maybe, and perhaps more importantly, success is being spiritually sound and leaving the world in a better place than what you found it.

Your definition of success may change over time, and that's okay. However, don't spend time doing anything that antagonizes your character and adversely affects others. Winning does not have to be a zero-sum game. This world is big enough for everyone to achieve a level of success and to equally share in its benefits. Success is not synonymous with money. Whatever your definition of success is, or may become, do not choose anything that will jeopardize your eternal soul.

2

BE TRUE TO YOURSELF

To find yourself learn to love yourself. – Debasish Mridha

You are a person and not a shredder. So quit tearing yourself to shred. – Scott Stabile

Accept yourself, love yourself, and keep moving forward. – Roy T. Bennet

"To thine own self be true" is one of many popular verses found in Louis Shakespeare's Hamlet.

What makes this verse so popular and what does it mean to be true to yourself?

THE PURSUIT OF TRUTH

Human beings have an insatiable desire to know facts, which I refer to as truth, and it begins at an early age. Young children exhibit this behavior by going through a period early in life, after learning to speak, when almost every phrase they utter is a question.

Where is Mommy?

Where is Daddy?

How old am I?

Where did I come from?

Question after question rolls off their tongue.

23

Mankind is constantly seeking to know the truth. The truth seems essential to our existence and survival. The field of science, and the study thereof, was created for this simple reason – to know the truth and to understand the hidden mysteries of the physical world. Because of our desire to know the truth – philosophy, the study of the fundamental nature of knowledge, reality, and existence, became an academic discipline.

Throughout earth's history, there have been periods of intellectual darkness and periods of enlightenment. The Age of Enlightenment, or the Age of Reason, brought forth the advancement of ideas like individual liberty, equality, constitutional government, and separation of church and state. It was the study of these ideas that led Thomas Jefferson, the writer of the United States Constitution, to pen the words – *We hold these truths to be self-evident: that all men are created equal; that they are endowed by their Creator with certain unalienable rights; that among these are life, liberty, and the pursuit of happiness.* Based on these words, in the absence of truth, mankind will lack knowledge of essential concepts that should be clear to everyone – that we are created beings and equal citizens on earth; that we have basic entitlements and rights, which includes the freedom to live life in the manner we choose, without oppressive restrictions; and most importantly, that we have the right to pursue the things in life that make us happy.

Why are human beings so inherently curious, constantly asking questions – seeking to know the truth?

Because our most innate desire is for freedom.

Without truth, we can never be free; without freedom, we can never be truly happy; and without happiness, life is difficult.

It was the desire for truth, to know both good and evil that caused our first parents, Adam and Eve, to eat from the forbidden tree. Believing that a deeper knowledge of truth was being withheld, Eve ate the forbidden fruit and gave some to her husband, and he ate it as well. After that fateful moment, everything changed for them, and for us. We lost our way, sacrificing our ability to have close, physical, face-to-face contact with our Creator. It's no surprise that the first words God spoke to the couple after they had eaten from the forbidden tree were, "Where are you?"

Adam responded by saying that he hid, but also that he was afraid because he was naked, something he was previously unaware of.

The majority of mankind has been spiritually hiding since this tragic moment unfolded; hiding behind false teachings, doctrines, and misguided science in an effort to cover up our true state – that we are naked and afraid without God. We have been striving to gain a broader knowledge of the terrestrial so that we are never again deceived regarding our current state of affairs. But just like a man fumbling around in the dark seeking to find his way, we must accept and believe the words of Jesus when he said, "I am the way, the truth, and the life." True freedom comes from knowing the truth – that Jesus loved us so much that he gave his life to restore the original relationship that man had with God, that was lost.

If your Creator loved you this much, you dishonor his sacrifice when you act in an unloving manner toward yourself by lying and pretending to be something you are not. You can lie to yourself, but you can't lie to God. He knows who you are and what you are. He knows your inner thoughts and most secret passions and desires. Despite this, He is not ashamed of you nor does he reject you.

BE HONEST WITH YOURSELF

You must be frank and honest with yourself if you desire full self-awareness and want to reach your maximum potential. In Psalms 51, David recognized that God requires that we have "truth in the inward parts" meaning that we must be honest with ourselves.

I was fortunate to learn this during my sophomore year in college. I was 19 years old with thoughts of becoming a mechanical engineer. However, I didn't always want to be an engineer. The seed for this pursuit was planted during my first year in high school. Prior to that, I wanted to be an accountant. Since I was six years old, I dreamed of going to work each day dressed in a navy-blue suit, a heavily starched white shirt, and a red tie while carrying a black leather briefcase. In my young mind, this is how an accountant dressed for work.

One day in high school, while sitting in algebra class, one of the school's guidance counselors dropped by and asked to speak with me outside the classroom. He was very excited to tell me about a college preparatory program that had just begun to encourage minority students to pursue careers in science and engineering. He told me that I was a good candidate for the program because of the high grades that I received in my previous math and science classes. I listened to his spiel half-heartedly, slightly curious in what he had to say. However, when he mentioned that the expected average starting salary for engineers at the time I would graduate college would be around

$40,000 a year, he had my full attention. I was 14 years old, and in 1989, this was a lot of money for a college graduate. In fact, at the time of this writing, depending on which city you live in, $40,000 a year is still an attractive starting salary for a college graduate. After our conversation, I had a new career in mind. I joined the program with visions of becoming an engineer one day.

For the next several years in high school, I took every math and science class that was available. I continued this pursuit with a steady focus, dreaming of the day when I would start college. That day finally arrived in the fall of 1992 when I enrolled at Morehouse College, a private, all-male, liberal arts, historically black college located in Atlanta, Georgia. Like many of the aspiring students in my class, I was a part of the dual degree engineering program. The program offered students the option of studying engineering through cooperative agreements with engineering schools throughout the country. Students in the program pursue either a general science curriculum or a major at Morehouse College for three or more years and then pursue a field of engineering at one of the participating engineering schools for two years. The program is commonly referred to as the "3-2" Program in Engineering, or simply the Dual-Degree Program in Engineering.

I continued in this program through my second year in college. For some reason, after receiving a C in Calculus I the prior semester, I still believed that I was fairly good at math and could continue taking more advanced classes. This fallacy ended when I hit a major roadblock in Calculus II. I studied hard to prepare for tests but could not achieve a grade better than a C. The professor teaching the class was very good. It wasn't his fault that I was performing poorly; it was mine – I was simply not talented enough in math to keep pace with the speed of the curriculum. I remember crying inconsolably one day after failing a test because I realized that my dream of becoming an engineer was probably not going to happen. I received a C minus in the class, which was not good enough to advance to Calculus III. If I wanted to continue as an engineering student, I would have to retake the class.

Regrettably, I did not continue my studies at Morehouse College but transferred to a university back home in Nebraska and changed my major to Business Administration with a concentration in Management Information Systems. I realized, if I continued to pursue engineering, I would be a C average student, at best. In truth, I could have stayed the course continuing to get C's, having to retake two or more classes along the way, and graduated with an engineering degree in six years like some of my former classmates. However, I realized continuing to take math classes was not the best use of my time. No matter how much I tried, I was never going to be gifted in math like some of the other students in my class. My talents lied elsewhere, and I finally reached a point when I was ready to accept my academic limitations.

It didn't take long to realize that changing my major was the right decision. My grades started to improve along with my confidence. Not long afterward, I was making the Dean's List each semester. In hindsight, I realized that I wanted to be an engineer for the wrong reasons. I was pursuing engineering because it was popular at the time – all the smart kids were doing it. I was also infatuated by the money I could make, not because I had a genuine love or passion for science. My motivation for becoming an engineer was misplaced.

I got a job as an Information Technology (IT) Consultant programming in COBOL during my last year of college. I did this for three years working mostly on Y2K projects. Y2K is a numeronym and was the common abbreviation for the year 2000 computer problem related to the formatting and storage of calendar data, that if not fixed, could cause havoc in computers and computer networks around the world at the beginning of the year 2000. The work was not entirely interesting, but it paid very well – enough to convince many former programmers to come out of retirement and many experienced programmers to delay their retirement date. I recall one Y2K project that I worked on when, at 24 years old, I was the youngest person on the project. Most of my co-workers were double my age and had some form of physical disability. One elderly woman needed the assistance of a walker to get around, one man wore a hearing aid, another guy had a lame hand after suffering a stroke, and another guy had only one lung from smoking too many cigarettes.

In hindsight, life was relatively good. I was making more money than most people I knew, let alone people my own age, and this gave me the financial freedom to live in a completely furnished two-bedroom apartment without needing a roommate to help pay the rent. I had a nice car and enough discretionary income to begin funding my 401(k). Despite the benefits that my job provided, I eventually became dissatisfied with the work. I was a good programmer, but I was not passionate about it. Once I left the office, I did not think about anything related to work until the next day.

COBOL is a high-level programming language for business applications. It was not the latest technology and there was little need for innovation. I tried to get contract assignments in other programming languages like C++, but because of the years of work experience I had accumulated programming in COBOL, my employer could charge a higher rate for my services and had little interest in trying to acquire assignments for me in other programming languages. Eventually, I left consulting to take a more permanent position with similar pay as a software engineer. Even this did not go as planned and seemed to lead to a dead-end career. Finally, I made the decision to leave IT and career switch by pursuing an MBA in finance and accounting at Vanderbilt University, which at the time was a Top 25 business school, as opposed to receiving a Master of Information Systems Management degree from Carnegie Mellon University, or attending Arizona State University where I could receive two degrees – an MBA and an MS in Information Technology. Oddly enough, with this decision, I was returning to my original childhood dream of entering a career in finance and accounting.

I graduated from business school in the spring of 2002 and the economy was still shaky from 9/11. This was not a good time to switch careers. Finding a job in finance was extremely difficult. Because of the financial hardship this caused, there were many occasions when I regretted pursuing an MBA and wished that I had gone to Carnegie Mellon instead. It took a few years, but I finally found a job that I really enjoyed working in the banking industry. I was able to use my knowledge of finance, accounting, and economics to make informed decisions and to properly analyze and evaluate a bank's financial performance and the effectiveness of the senior management team. No longer did I dread going to work every day. Not only did I enjoy my job, but I was also extremely good at it, gaining the respect of my peers, co-workers, and the staff at the banks that I examined as a bank regulator.

Sometimes, your first mind is your right mind. My subconscious knew what was best for me and created the urge to pursue a career in finance and accounting. A tiny voice inside my head directed me towards the path I was to pursue. Instead of listening to this internal voice, I allowed external voices to distract me, leading me to pursue engineering instead.

I now recognize that internal voice as the whispers of the Holy Spirit.

In order to discern the Holy Spirit's voice, I had to recognize the methods by which the Holy Spirit speaks. There are few people fortunate enough to actually hear God's voice, such as when God spoke directly to Abraham and Moses. In most cases, the Holy Spirit speaks through your internal inclinations, and when you fail to acknowledge His soft, subtle voice, the Holy Spirit may resort to speaking through your circumstances, such as in the case of Jonah when his disobedience landed him in the belly of a fish.

Whenever you have an idea that solves a problem or you feel an ongoing urge to complete a specific task, that once completed will uplift humanity, this is the voice of the Holy Spirit – a voice that will never encourage you to do something that is contrary to the Word of God or His law.

The reason why it's so difficult to discern the Holy Spirit's voice is that our inherent sinful nature is constantly fighting against our Godly spirit. Paul alluded to the realism of this struggle when he said,

> "I don't really understand myself, for I want to do what is right, but I don't do it. Instead, I do what I hate. But if I know what I am doing is wrong, this shows that I agree that the

law is good. So I am not the one doing wrong; it is sin living in me that does it" (Romans 7:14-20).

Many times, your sinful nature and urges are so strong it prevents you from hearing your Creator's voice and recognizing when He is speaking to you.

God is gentle. When He speaks to you, He doesn't raise his voice, shout, or scream. He speaks softly, subtly at first, and then gradually raises the volume if you fail to acknowledge His will. Finally, as a last resort, He is able to gain your full attention by speaking to you through your circumstances, which usually comes after you find yourself in an undesirable situation caused by your own actions. If you are quick to discern and heed His original suggestion, you can save yourself from losing time and experiencing a lot of heartache and pain.

I had to learn this the hard way.

I previously mentioned I had a choice of attending Vanderbilt University (Vanderbilt), Arizona State University (Arizona State), or Carnegie Mellon University (Carnegie Mellon). In hindsight, second to choosing whom to marry, this was probably the most important decision I had made to this point due to the direction my life would take and the effect it had on shaping my character, mindset, and beliefs.

I applied to six business schools, but I was placed on many of the school's *waitlist*. The *waitlist* is extended to candidates whose application is not as strong as more desirable students but is still worthy of consideration.

A good friend of mine, with a similar application profile, was also applying to business schools but chose only to apply to schools ranked in the top 10 whereas my choices were less ambitious. Wisely, he also applied to a one-year program offered by Carnegie Mellon to receive a Master of Information Systems Management degree. Unfortunately, he was not accepted to any of the business schools he applied to but was accepted into the program at Carnegie Mellon, which was ranked #2 at the time behind The Massachusetts Institute of Technology (MIT). He enrolled and started school in January. Meanwhile, I was still waiting for an admission decision.

In late April, my friend encouraged me to apply to the same program at Carnegie Mellon. Since we had similar application profiles, I had a good chance of being accepted too. I examined the application process and discovered the application deadline had passed. My friend told me to speak with someone from the admissions office. Perhaps they would be willing to make an exception and accept a late application. The worst thing they could say is no. Having nothing to lose, I called the university and spoke with a woman from the Admissions Office. I told her a friend of mine was enrolled and that he spoke very highly of the program, and that I was interested in attending as well. Additionally, I told her that I had previously applied to Carnegie Mellon's business school and was currently on the *waitlist*. The admissions officer told me since I had already paid an application fee, they could accept my application to the business school as proof of my intent to attend Carnegie Mellon. She told me that she would walk across campus to the business school, scan the application on file, and use it as an application to the Heinz School Master of Information Systems Management program. One week later, during the first week of May, I received an email offering me acceptance into the program! One week later, I was offered a small scholarship to help defray the cost of tuition! One week later, I received an acceptance letter from Arizona State;

however, the offer did not include a scholarship and it was the lowest ranked of all the schools that I had applied. Meanwhile, I was still waiting to receive an admission decision from the other business school that I had applied.

At this point, I was ready to join my friend and start school in August at Carnegie Mellon. In my mind, attending Carnegie Mellon was better than going to Arizona State. I made a trip to Pittsburgh to visit the school and to look for accommodation. Shortly thereafter, I received a phone call from the Head of Admissions at Vanderbilt offering acceptance into their MBA program. I thanked him for the offer but told him that I had already accepted an offer to attend a master's program at Carnegie Mellon and that their offer came with a scholarship. He asked if I would forward him the email that I received. A few days later, he phoned me and said that he would match Carnegie Mellon's offer of aid. He then went on to suggest, that although the program at Carnegie Mellon was quite good, the degrees where not the same and that an MBA was far more versatile than a Master of Information Systems Management and would prove more valuable in the long run.

His argument was very convincing; but honestly, he had me when he said Vanderbilt would match the financial aid package. I had my heart set on getting an MBA, anyway. I wanted to move away from information technology and I saw this as my chance. Plus, at the time, MBAs were receiving lofty pay packages from companies. In many cases, graduates were doubling their pre-MBA salary and this was in addition to the hiring bonuses they received. I accepted his offer and informed Carnegie Mellon that I would not be attending.

I sincerely enjoyed the two years I attended Vanderbilt. I learned a considerable amount of information in a short time and was introduced to some amazing, smart, hardworking students and made some friendships that I still enjoy to this day. The only unfortunate thing about my time spent there was the timing. Shortly into my second year in the MBA program, something happened that very few people in the United States, and maybe the world, will never forget.

I was exercising in the school's gymnasium on September 11, 2001, when a plane struck one of the World Trade Center towers. The students in the gym started to gather around the televisions near the treadmills and exercise bikes to watch the news and to witness the events unfolding. Like many people, I thought the plane crash was an accident. When a second plane struck the other tower, I knew it was no accident.

The effects of 9/11 went beyond the victims, and the many heroes, that lost their lives on that tragic day – it affected the overall economy driving the country into a recession. Many of the companies that had scheduled on-campus interviews canceled. Some companies began to rescind job offers that were extended at the completion of the summer internship. Unfortunately, our career planning and placement office was slow to respond to this crisis and gave little assistance to worried students who were anxious to secure a job before graduation. The number of students able to secure a job before graduation was above 85% for the class of 2001; however, the percentage dropped below 60% for my class, and I was included in this figure. It took me over a year to find a job. At first, I tried to find a finance job in investment banks. After a few months with no success, I expanded my search to include any company offering a job in finance. I was fortunate to get several interviews, but the result was always the same – a call or a rejection letter from a recruiter saying that I will not be offered a job. After a few months of getting rejected for finance positions, I tried to get a job programming in COBOL again, but the glory days of Y2K were over and companies had slashed their IT budgets or were not planning any new development projects. I was miserable. I didn't have a job, I had no income, and my money was quickly running out.

Meanwhile, my good friend that went to Carnegie Mellon was doing great. He graduated prior to 9/11 and received a high paying job from a world-renowned IT company. In his adult life outside of college, he has never had a day where he was unemployed. To this day, even after attending a Top 25 business school, I doubt that my annual salary has ever matched or exceeded his.

I can't say with absolute certainty that had I attended Carnegie Mellon my experience would have mirrored my friend's. However, given the strength of an IT degree from Carnegie Mellon coupled with the robust demand for skilled IT professionals, I doubt that I would have been unemployed as long as I was. In the end, approximately three years after leaving Vanderbilt, I did reach a point when I was satisfied with my career, the work I was doing, and the amount of money I was making. However, I can't ignore the fact that I lost three years of salaried income during this period – two years to complete business school and one year looking for a job. Had I attended Carnegie Mellon instead, and graduated prior to 9/11, it is very likely that I would have been the recipient of a high salary and a large signing bonus while missing only one year of salaried income.

I mention this experience not to reflect or cry over "spilled milk", but to illustrate the harmful effects of going against God's will. Without a doubt, I most certainly believe that

I ended up where I was destined regardless of which graduate program I attended, but the path that I took to get to where I am currently in life could have been much easier and with less hardship along the way.

When a person travels to reach a predetermined destination, there are usually multiple ways to get there. The best path to take is often the shortest. The shortest path will generally take less time because the distance traveled is shorter. Unless there are obstacles along the way that slow your progress, this will remain true. Since time is money, the path that takes the least amount of time to travel is the most optimal.

Divine Providence made it extremely easy for me to attend Carnegie Mellon – a closed-door remarkably opened. Unlike the business schools that I applied to, the admissions committee did not hesitate to make a decision by putting me on a *waitlist*. They used an application on file at another campus graduate program as their own and granted me admission within a week. Not only was I accepted into the program after the application period had expired, I was awarded a scholarship. This was God's way of telling what to do – that the best path was for me to attend Carnegie Mellon instead of Vanderbilt. Unfortunately, I was too immature to recognize and understand the manner in which God speaks to me.

God reserves the right to speak to you in any manner He chooses. It's your job to recognize the method God uses. For my friend, God spoke to him through his circumstance. God made the decision easy by giving him only two choices – attend Carnegie Mellon or keep working and try gaining admission to a top-ranked business program the following year.

God used my situation to speak to me too, although mine was slightly more complicated because it included three choices – attend one of the three graduate programs that I was offered admission: Carnegie Mellon, Arizona State, or Vanderbilt. Nevertheless, the real decision wasn't a matter of which school I would attend, rather whose voice I would listen to – God's voice, evident by the remarkable manner in which the Carnegie Mellon admission decision was made; or man's voice, the slow Johnny-come-lately offer of acceptance from Vanderbilt that came after being placed on the *waitlist*. It's evident which of us, my friend or I, listened to God's voice and made the better decision. My friend's journey was short and less difficult while mine was longer and more cumbersome. If only I had listened and known then what I know now.

I learned a great deal from this experience.

LESSON #1

It taught me that God speaks to me through my circumstances and that my current situation will usually dictate what action I should take, if any. It also let me know if God has endorsed my plans with his favor. When everything I need to make my venture successful comes relatively easy, meaning there is very little I am required to do, I know that this is God speaking to me. Notice very carefully that I said I am still required to contribute in some way, even if my contribution is small. God is not a genie in a bottle that grants your wishes by doing everything you ask without you doing anything in return. This would make you lazy and it goes against God's principle that man was made to work. I offer as proof of these statements the miraculous way the Israelites escaped 400 years of bondage in Egypt. They did not have to protest, riot, or wage war against the Egyptians. They did not have to raise one finger in their own defense. All they had to do was gather their belongings, follow instructions, and walk out of Egypt.

What is for you, is for you. All you have to do is follow instructions and the path in front of you, no matter how scary it may seem, trusting that you will receive everything you need along your journey.

LESSON #2

I learned that ignoring God's voice would most certainly result in unnecessary misery because He always has your best interest in mind. Jeremiah 29:11 says, "For surely I know the plans I have for you, says the Lord, plans for your welfare and not for harm, to give you a future with hope." God is omnipresent. His thoughts and plans are far superior to yours. God wanted to make this clear so he led the prophet Isaiah to write,

> "For my thoughts are not your thoughts, neither are your ways my ways. For as the heaves are higher than the earth, so are my ways higher than your ways, and my thoughts than yours" (Isaiah 55:8-9).

Ignoring God's suggestions has consequences and will bring about an unfavorable outcome. Therefore, never make an improvident decision by rejecting what God is telling you, or offering you.

God never takes away your choice. He gives you free will and allows you to make your own decisions. This doesn't mean that you should not seek His approval for major decisions. Indeed, you should. When it comes to things that can materially impact your life, and that of others, you should seek to hear from your Creator. He will not disappoint you. He will direct you to the right path.

When God orders your steps, you need to be ready to move your feet; otherwise, you may forfeit your reward. There are times when you must take a bold step forward to accept what God has for you even when your footing seems uncertain or when what He has for you doesn't match your current plans. For example, in the Old Testament, there were two occasions when the Israelites had to pass through a large body of water – once when they crossed the Red Sea as they fled Egypt and the next when they crossed the river Jordan to enter the Promised Land. Each event was probably incredibly scary. However, in order to benefit they had to be willing to move forward.

I challenge you to keep moving forward.

Chapter Summary

You owe it to yourself to be truly honest with yourself – about the type of person you are, your abilities, your strengths and weaknesses, and what really motivates you. This is the first step in your journey for truth. Verity brings self-awareness, acceptance of who you are – and with this comes freedom. Truth in the "inward parts" helps bring about personal ownership of life decisions – decisions that, hopefully, lead to success stories and not the experience of failure and regret.

If you are not completely honest with yourself regarding your natural talents, abilities, intellect, shortcomings, bad habits, etc., you can bring upon yourself the hopelessness of an explorer traveling without a compass; every road or path will appear to be the right one. You may eventually find your destination, but only after long and unnecessary detours that are often very painful to experience. Be careful of misguided motives, for this can lead you down the wrong path causing you to make bad decisions that can sometimes take years to correct.

Your first mind is often your correct mind. The inward inclination you feel will sometimes seem like a soft voice that is offering you advice or direction for an important life-changing decision. Listen to this voice because it will not betray you. It is not self-serving or motivated by greed. It always has your best interest in mind. This voice may be difficult to discern, but you must learn to recognize this voice and block out the noise that is there to distract and prevent you from hearing your Creator.

When you are on the right path, things will begin to fall into place. Problems, when they occur, and they will, will not be impossible to overcome. With any journey you undertake, you will reach your destination if you continue to move forward.

3

DISCOVER YOUR PURPOSE

There is no failure except failure to serve one's purpose. – Henry Ford

Believe in your heart that you're meant to live a life full of passion, purpose, magic, and miracles. – Roy T. Bennett

Find a purpose to serve, not a lifestyle to live. – Criss Jami

You are not an accident. You are not a mistake. You are of great value. Your existence was contemplated by your Creator long before your father and mother knew each other. Your Creator is intimately aware of who you are and every aspect of your life. While speaking about your Creator's concern for you Jesus said, "But the very hairs of your head are all numbered" (Matthew 10:30). Nothing happens to you without His knowledge. Your life, your happiness, your prosperity is of great importance to Him. There is a reason why you are here. There is a divine purpose for your life.

THE REASON WE WORK

God did not create mankind with the intent that we should be idle. Moments after Adam was created God gave him something to do. He brought the animals before Adam to see what he would call them and whatever Adam called them that was their name. Naming animals was not Adam's only responsibility. He and his wife, Eve, were also responsible for the Garden of Eden's upkeep and maintenance. The couple had six days to work and one day to rest. Most of the world still follows their example.

Work is the will of God. King Solomon said,

> "There is nothing better than to enjoy food and drink and to find satisfaction in work. Then I realized that these pleasures are from the hand of God" (Ecclesiastes 2:24).

Solomon later said, "For God gives wisdom and knowledge and joy to a man who is good in His sight" (Ecclesiastes 2: 26).

What does "good" mean?

Good means pleasing in His sight.

Men and woman that use their God-given talents by doing something for which they are best suited are pleasing to God. Their work is a form of worship and a benevolent act of service. Not surprisingly, they are generally more knowledgeable, capable, and happier than someone that is not using their natural talent. They have a competitive advantage over others. Work does not feel like work. A person that is working in a field for which they are not suited, perhaps only working for money, does not take pleasure in their work. To them, work is as burdensome as "gathering and collecting"; and in the end, the work they do will be so "that he may give to him who is good before God" (Ecclesiastes 2:26).

KNOW YOURSELF

You are a work of art – a masterpiece like no other. Although there may be similarities between you and others, there has never been anyone exactly like you, and there never will be. You are as unique as your fingerprint. That said, the path you set for yourself in life should be your path and not the path of someone else.

You have a work for which you are best suited. However, you are not born into this world with a user manual; therefore, it is entirely up to you to figure out the work you should do. God gave you free will. He is not going to tell you what to do with your life. What you do is entirely up to you. This is the way it should be. Human beings are not robots programmed to follow orders.

There are times when it is wise for you to follow the path of someone that has walked the same path before. You should seek these individuals as guides and emulate their behavior, work ethic, and overall professionalism. However, the choice to walk their path needs to be your own choosing. To allow someone else to make this decision for you is folly. Although mentors may have your best interest in mind, they may not always recognize and consider your God-given abilities, which is the source of the competitive advantage you have over others.

Your God-given abilities are what define you – they are the substance that drives your innermost desires that seek expression. The desire you have to paint, write, sing, dance, run, motivate, lead, inspire, etc., comes from your God-given abilities fighting to be released. You would be wise to trust and obey these internal urges because they are the source of your greatness.

Sometimes your internal urge or desire is not consistent with your natural ability.

Consider two famous athletes: Michael Jordan and Tim Tebow.

Many people consider Michael Jordan to be the greatest basketball player of all time. After winning three consecutive championships for the Chicago Bulls, he decided to retire from basketball and pursue a professional career in baseball – a sport he played as a child. Unfortunately, his stint as a minor league baseball player did not go well. The greatest basketball player in the world was not as good at baseball. With all due respect to Mr. Jordan, he was never going to make it to the Major League no matter how competitive his nature or how much he practiced. He simply lacked the athletic ability and natural talent needed to advance beyond playing in the minor leagues. Favorably, Mr. Jordan gave up his pursuit of playing baseball and returned to basketball. He then led the Chicago Bulls to another three consecutive championships.

Tim Tebow is incredibly talented and was a highly successful college football player. As the quarterback for the University of Florida's football team, Tebow won individual and team awards, including the Heisman Trophy which is awarded annually to the most outstanding player in college football, and the College Football Bowl Championship Series (BCS) National Championship twice (2006, 2008). He was selected in the first round of the 2009 National Football League (NFL) draft by the Denver Broncos. Many NFL coaches and owners believed Tebow would do well in the NFL and would be an asset to any football organization, but not everyone was a believer.

Tebow, despite his impressive physical size and athleticism, lacked certain throwing mechanics that are necessary for playing the quarterback position in the NFL, where the play is more competitive and the opposing defenses are much faster. Sadly, the naysayers were right. Tebow played only three full seasons in the NFL – two with the Denver Broncos and one with the New York Jets. Tebow worked extremely hard to correct his throwing mechanics and accuracy, but he did not improve enough to convince the general managers and coaches for the last two teams he suited up for to add him to the team's 53-man active roster.

Without question, Tebow is a strong competitor and an extremely hard worker. His athleticism powered him to succeed in high school and in college. However, he could not overcome his throwing flaws and inaccuracy, which were too deep for the NFL, particularly at quarterback, which is the only position he was willing to play. At the time of this writing, Tebow is pursuing a career in professional baseball, another sport he excelled at in high school. Time will tell if this pursuit is more successful. I wish him the best.

In life, you are never going to please everyone. You are going to be criticized, so you might as well do what you love. However, there is what you WANT to do and what you CAN do. Like the famous quote in Shakespeare's *Hamlet*, "To thine own self be true." Do not doubt yourself and your chance for success, but do not fool yourself into thinking you are something that you are not, especially if you have talents that are more suited for something else. More will be said about this in a later chapter.

EMBRACE NOBLE PURSUITS

You are allowed to pursue whatever occupation you want as long as it does not violate God's moral law, the Ten Commandments, which are summarized into two simple love commandments.

> "You shall love the Lord your God with all your heart, with all your soul, and with all your mind. This is the first and great commandment. A second is equally important: 'Love your neighbor as yourself'" (Matthew 22:37-39).

God is not overly concerned with your choice of occupation as long as it does not violate a moral law or pose a physical threat to your personal safety and the people around you. Consider a child that ask their mother if they can go outside to play. The child has the freedom to choose whatever game they want as long as it is safe; it will not harm them or someone else. As long as they follow this rule, they do not have to ask their mother what game to play. The mother is not overly concerned with what game the child chooses as long as it is safe and the child stays within a defined boundary that is deemed safe for them to play in. In time, the child will learn which games they enjoy playing most. Just like the mother in this example, God has established boundaries (Ten Commandments) to keep you safe.

The first of the two love commandments says, "You shall love the Lord your God with all your heart, with all your soul, and with all your mind." Said differently, you are to love God using your complete being – which includes your heart, soul, and mind.

The heart represents the entire body, for it's the continuous beating of this organ that pushes oxygen-filled blood through your veins, keeping all parts of your body alive. The soul is the breath of life poured into you by your Creator; it's a unique substance that makes you an individual. The soul, when combined with your physical body, is what makes you a living soul (Genesis 2:7). A new soul comes into existence whenever a child is conceived. The mind is the vessel that houses your spirit, and that spirit is your thoughts, desires, emotions, character, and combination of skills and abilities; this is why you can have a holy spirit or an evil spirit.

The body without a soul is not living; the soul outside the body can do nothing physical; and a mind without the capacity

48

to think, desire, and feel is useless. Therefore, to obey the two love commandments requires your body, soul, and mind all work together.

The command states, "You shall love." While love is described as *a feeling or emotion*; to show love requires activity – it requires you to do something. Whether you realize it or not, using your God-given abilities is an act of love to your Creator, and He takes pleasure in seeing you use your gifts.

Why would you choose an occupation or job that does not utilize the God-given abilities that make you unique, that give you a competitive advantage?

That is like a close friend or family member giving you a gift made specifically for you that you never use.

Do Not Be Motivated By Money

Money is a strong motivator that can work for the good and the detriment of society. The need to support oneself, particularly if the place or environment where the person lives embrace the notion that if you don't work you don't eat, will cause a lazy person to become a contributor to society. Often, the joy of the job is not what compels people to work but simply the need to earn money.

For the sake of honesty, there are numerous "dirty jobs" that would never be done if it were not for the fact that someone is being paid to do it. The same is true for professional occupations, and this can work against society. In the United States, there are countless medical professionals who lack a bedside manner but are in the profession because of the higher salaries that are paid. The desire for more money pushes some doctors to rush through the medical visit and diagnosis in order to get to the next co-pay, instead of patiently listening to the patient's concerns and problems, and in the more severe cases, provide a false diagnosis so the patient can come back for more unnecessary treatments. Even more costly to society, is that there are numerous misplaced, unmotivated teachers that are put in charge of shaping young impressionable minds. Sadly, these individuals are only in the profession because they need the money or they enjoy having their summers off.

Everyone is entitled to make a living in the job they choose, but it should not come at the expense of others. If you are working in a job in which you are not fully dedicated and are not giving 100%, it's time for you to find another job where you can be more committed.

There is a tremendous difference between a "job done" and a "job well done." You would not want to live in a building where the contractor cut corners and did not build according to code to save time and to reduce costs. The problems that can occur later can be quite costly to resolve, and dangerous if not corrected. That said, whenever someone sets out to only "do the job" instead of trying to do "a good job", the outcome is generally less than satisfactory.

The work you do is a service to society. Society needs your best work in order to function properly. When you fail to provide the best service possible, you rob society by not fully contributing to its betterment. In fact, you are working against your own interest. Consider what would happen if everyone decided to not give 100%.

Many loving parents push their children to become doctors, dentists, and engineers because these professions pay higher salaries, whereas their children may want to pursue a career in writing, teaching, or social work. The parents mean well, believing that their choice of profession is in their child's best interest. Nevertheless, parents that force their children to pursue a particular occupation are short-sighted. They don't understand that if your choice of work is aligned with your God-given talent, the money will eventually come (you may have to learn how to be more creative) and that you'll be happier in the long run.

In most cases, your talent will make a way for itself. Just remember that hard work beats talent when talent fails to work hard.

NEVER STOP WORKING

Once you discover your purpose and commit your life to it, then you should continue doing it indefinitely. There is no reason for you to retire just because you have made enough money or because you have grown old. If you enjoy the work and are still able to do it, keep doing it. If you must, reduce the amount of time that you work. Take a less active role or a consultative approach. Mentor someone by passing along the knowledge that you have accumulated over the years. But please, do not stop working and rob the world of your unique gift.

We all have a role to play in the world. You are a part of something bigger than yourself. Until the time comes when you take your last breath, you should strive to function as a true citizen of the earth by contributing to its betterment.

In a way, we are all like members of a large ant colony. There is much you can learn from observing ants. Consider the ways that an ant colony functions. Each ant is part of a collective whole, with each having a specific task to perform to support the colony. Because each role is important and necessary to ensure the colony's survival, no role is more important than another. The queen supports the colony's survival by laying millions of eggs. Without the queen, there wouldn't be new ants to replace those that have died. The soldier ant's job is to protect the colony from predators and to use their strength and large jaws to carry large objects. The drones are the only male ants in the colony. Without them, there wouldn't be any ants to mate with the princess ants, the winged unfertilized virgin queens that will someday fly out to create new colonies. The worker ants, or simply the "workers", are the most common ants found in the colony. Their job is to look after the unhatched eggs, dig tunnels, and locate food and bring it back to the nest.

The Bible recognizes ant's tireless effort and labor to gather food during the summer for the winter months that lie ahead (Proverbs 6:6, Proverbs 30:25). A fact that is not well known is that the lifespan of a worker ant is not that long, only a few months sometimes. Therefore, the food that they gather over the summer is not for them to eat, it's for the ants that will be born later!

What an incredible display of unselfish behavior – working to benefit others when you will not be able to receive any immediate benefit yourself.

At no point during an ant's life do they stop working. They work until the day they die. Ants spend their entire lives working for the good of the colony.

Aren't human beings smarter and wiser than ants?

Shouldn't you continue to use your talents and abilities for the good of future generations?

Indeed, you have a moral obligation to continue to use your God-given abilities for as long as you physically and mentally can.

If not for several moral reasons, consider the large financial incentive as proof of why you should continue working. The longer you work the more wealth you can accumulate for future generations and for philanthropy. Capital is not finite. It will diminish unless you continue to add to it.

If you don't need the money, don't spend your golden years of life working to build "bigger barns" for yourself like the parable of the rich fool (Luke 12:16-21). Instead, use the money to bless others. The sick and poor will always be with us. A large percentage of these sufferers are children. Your dollars can go a long way in relieving some of their pain.

CHAPTER SUMMARY

You were created to work. You have a specific job to do. By dutifully using your God-given talents, you honor your Creator and uplift humanity.

Always remember to be true to yourself. If you must work (and you should) do something that is aligned with your natural ability and God-given talent. Embrace noble pursuits that can be a blessing to you and others. Don't choose a profession or an occupation solely for the money. You may derive short-term benefits from this, but it will prove to be a long-term mistake that you will later regret.

Never stop working as long as you are physically and mentally able. You have a moral obligation to uplift humanity with your talents and labor for as long as you can. Remember how unselfishly ants labor. They ensure the survival of future generations by working all summer storing food for the winter months that lie ahead, even though the ants that gather the food will not be alive to eat it.

4

USE IT OR LOSE IT

Our talents are the gift that God gave us...What we make of our talents is our gift back to God. – Leo Buscaglia

Talent is a wonderful thing, but it won't carry a quitter. – Stephen King

Talent is a word lazy people use to explain why they can't do things. – Edmund McMillen

You have been endowed by your Creator with talents, gifts, and natural abilities. In His wisdom, He created diversity. Although all human beings are equally loved and valued, we were not individually given the same number of gifts and do not have the same capabilities. While some may believe this truth to be unfair, it remains a fact of life. Instead of being frustrated, angry, bitter and coveting the natural abilities that were given to someone else, it would be a better use of time to focus on your own abilities and how you are deploying them. For if you are not adequately using the talents and abilities you currently possess, then it's a waste of time thinking about how unfair it is that someone else has more talents and abilities than you do.

Don't make the mistake of believing that having more gifts and natural abilities come without a price. Jesus, when speaking to his disciples, said, "When someone has been given much, much will be required in return; and when someone has been entrusted with much, even more will be required" (Luke 12:48). In fact, if what you are given is not used adequately, it will be taken from you and redistributed to someone that is more capable and deserving of the gift.

USE IT OR LOSE IT

The proof of the preceding statement is made clear in a story Jesus told called *The Parable of the Talents* that appears in Matthew 25. In the story, a man traveling to a far country gives his servants some of his goods before departing. To the first servant he gives five talents of gold, to the second he gives two, and to the third, he gives only one, each according to his own ability to manage them. The servant who received five talents went and invested them in the market and made another five talents. Likewise, the servant that was given two talents gained two more also. But the servant that received only one talent, instead of trading it like the other two, dug a hole and buried it in the ground, and hid his master's money. When the man returned from his journey, he settled accounts with them to see what they had done.

The two servants who increased the number of talents in their possession were commended and rewarded for their stewardship. For the servant that hid his master's money in the ground, there was a strong rebuke, "You wicked and lazy servant!...why didn't you deposit my money in the bank? At least I could have gotten some interest on it" (Matthew 25:27). The one talent this servant had was taken from him and given to the servant that had ten talents. Jesus would conclude this story by saying,

> "To those who use well what they are given, even more will be given, and they will have abundance. But for those who do nothing, even what little they have will be taken away" (Matthew 25:29).

This simple parable powerfully explains the difference in ideology between those that will become rich and those that will remain poor. The first and second servant took what they were given and used it to create more. Neither complained about the amount they were given nor how it might be unfair that they were not given more. Nor did they complain about their circumstance. They both went to work using only what they were given. Through hard work, diligence, and thoughtfulness, both were profitable – doubling the amount they started with. If their master had extended the duration of his journey their results probably would have been even more successful. This is what is meant by, "He will have abundance." The servant that was given only one talent, and who made no effort to increase what little he already possessed, even that was taken away. Therefore, he ended up with less than what he started with.

How many times have you seen this happen, someone becoming poorer than what they were previously?

How many times have you heard the success story of immigrants migrating to the United States for a better life seeking to build something sustainable for themselves and their posterity, only to later hear about an entitled, more apathetic second and third generation who lack similar work ethic, fail to capitalize on their predecessor's hard work?

Instead of improving their socioeconomic status, they end up moving backward.

The two faithful servants that increased their master's wealth were not greedy men; they were simply motivated by increase. There is nothing wrong with wanting increase – wanting more. The desire for more is the desire for a richer, fuller, and more abundant life. This desire is praiseworthy, as illustrated in the parable above, as long as your gain does not result in someone else being exploited or taken advantage of. The man who does not desire to live more abundantly is abnormal, perplexing, and actually quite bizarre.

Although this parable concerns money and shows that investing, and not hoarding, if used for godly purposes is commendable, this fact is confused because the word talent (in modern English) has come to mean skills or abilities. Regardless of whether you believe this parable is referring to money or natural abilities, one point is true – anything that is not put to use will diminish over time. God created this natural law. It's true for money, muscles, mental ability, and for all human virtues. Ambition, if not used declines. Faith, unused diminishes. Love, if not expressed weakens. Lack of use causes loss. Anything that you do not employ by putting to good use, you forfeit. Said differently, whatever you don't use, you lose.

If you lack something, you can turn your deficiency into abundance – but this begins with using what you already have. You have to put to work what you currently possess. There is no substitute for industry. Your Creator is not going to say, "Well planned, good and faithful servant." He will not say well thought, well said, or well strategized either. There is one commendation, "Well done, good and faithful servant."

Whatever your Creator has put in your heart to do, take action to get it done. Do not hesitate. Make good use of the time that you are given. Every minute of time that is not used wisely is wasted. Every minute is valuable. To make this point clearer, I draw your attention to a poem written by Benjamin E. Mays that I heard for the first time when I was a student at Morehouse College.

JUST A MINUTE

I've only just a minute,
Only sixty seconds in it.
Forced upon me, didn't choose it,
But it's up to me to use it.
I must suffer if I lose it,
Give an account if I abuse it,
Just a tiny little minute,
But eternity is in it.

Ask yourself, how much time do you waste?

Too much, if you answer honestly.

Stop wasting time.

Your Creator has already given you the tools to be successful. You already possess everything you need.

WHAT IS THAT IN YOUR HAND

Everything has potential that allows it to become something more than its current use.

You have vast potential even when your current situation is not very favorable.

What matters most is what you do with your potential because potential without action will never produce results.

Consider a 19-year old, seven feet tall Maasai warrior that has a 38-inch vertical leap, who dreams of playing professional basketball but lives in a village in Kenya. This young man has vast potential. Indeed, he can become many noble things: a good herdsman, father, and later a tribal chief. But imagine him on an NBA basketball court causing havoc – slam-dunking on opponents, blocking shots, and aggressively rebounding. No doubt, he would be highly compensated for his athletic prowess, earning more in one year than what his entire village could earn in a hundred. If he were to repatriate even half his earnings back home, he could raise the quality of life for his village while enjoying a high standard of living for himself. But in order for this to happen, he must see opportunity beyond his current environment and use. Using this example, we can conclude that potential, if it is to receive maximum results, must also be rightly placed.

The greatest inhibitor to any individual advancing is not poverty, war, slavery, or disease; it's lack of imagination and an even more terrible mental barricade called excuses. Excuses have hindered personal development more than anything else known to man because it removes personal responsibility and accountability. Anyone can come up with numerous reasons why something cannot be done. But 9 times out of 10, the "reason" is not a reason at all, it's an "excuse", and there is a big difference between the two. The difference is in accountability.

Take any student as an example. Common excuses for why students fail include:

- The teacher was terrible and made the tests too difficult
- My classmates were noisy and kept distracting me
- I did not have enough time to complete class work

The list of possible excuses is endless. There are as many excuses for failure as there are failing grades. However, if a person were to take accountability for their decisions and their actions, then the excuses would be seen as the real reasons for failure. Accountability would look like this:

- I did not seek additional help to better understand the concepts that were taught

- I did not request to be seated somewhere else or near the front of the class to avoid getting distracted

- I spend too much time playing video games or talking on the phone instead of doing my coursework

You probably notice a trend here. For every excuse the student makes for why they failed the class, there is a real reason that points to something they did or did not do. In most other situations in life, the excuse provided is related to something they did not have or is due to unforeseen circumstances.

Consider the poem below that is committed to memory by many fraternities and sororities:

Excuses, excuses, excuses! Excuses are tools of incompetence used to build monuments of nothingness and those who indulge in their uses are seldom capable of anything else. Excuses...excuses...excuses!

Let's go back to our Maasai warrior living in a Kenyan village. Undoubtedly, many in his village can come up with numerous "reasons" why he should stay in his current state. But what if, instead of guarding livestock and taking photos with visiting tourist, he actively sought out the best basketball coach in Kenya?

No doubt, leaving his village may not be an easy undertaking. The road forward can be full of potholes to disrupt his progress. First, he will have to leave home and family and abandon tribal life to live in the city, and once a coach is located – engage in numerous hours of practice each day to develop the footwork and agility required for basketball. But the most difficult obstacle to overcome is not any of these aforementioned challenges; it's all the excuses, camouflaged as reasons, for why he should not leave his village.

Instead of the prior hypothetical example, let's review the life of a person most people are familiar with – the life of the prophet Moses. This story allows us to assess the debilitating power of excuses and recognize the chains excuses place on us.

The events that led to Moses leaving Egypt were unfortunate. He saw a slave being beaten and came to his defense by killing his assailant. As a result, Moses had to flee Egypt in order to save his life. After spending 40 years in the desert, Moses was no longer the man he used to be. He has changed. Once a proud prince and bold defender of his people and anyone he saw being assaulted, he has morphed into a passive man whose only interest was looking after sheep. The time in the desert had caused his former self, that willingness to come to the aid of a defenseless slave, to evaporate like water on a hot summer day.

One day while attending to his flock of sheep, he saw a miracle. A bush burned with fire but was not consumed. Curious, Moses climbs the mountain to see this burning bush and is approached by God. Moses is told that he is being sent to Egypt to free his people from bondage. The response Moses gives is very revealing and provides a window for us to see how much he has changed. Moses says, "Who am I to appear before Pharaoh? Who am I to lead the people of Israel out of Egypt" (Exodus 3:11).

As a Hebrew that once lived in the palace, there were few more qualified and better suited for this task. Moses was the son of a Hebrew slave and the adopted son of Pharaoh's daughter. He could relate to the hard life of a Hebrew and the easy life of an Egyptian. Yet Moses' response shows that he had forgotten who he was and had lost his former identity. He had become a victim of life due to an unfortunate event. Instead of living and planning for what the future could be, he was just getting on with life. He had become a simple man with no ambition beyond looking after sheep. When he was presented with an opportunity to be the leader of something great, instead of happily accepting, he responds with several excuses for why he is not the right man for the job. He even begs God to send someone else (Exodus 4:13).

God assures him that He will be with him every step of the way and finally asks Moses what appears to be an odd question, "What is that in your hand?" (Exodus 4:2).

Moses responds by saying, "A rod."

The rod Moses held was typical of the time and his profession. The rod was most likely used for walking, guiding sheep to walk in the right direction, and to occasionally fend off a wild animal. But notice what happens to the rod once Moses accepts the mission given to him and set outs to return to Egypt. In Exodus 4:20 it is no longer referred to as a rod, it is now the "rod of God." This rod is later used by Moses to perform incredible miracles, whereas before it was only an ordinary stick.

Just like Moses, as well as modern-day leaders such as Oprah Winfrey, Indra Nooyi, Melinda Gates, Jeff Bezos, LeBron James, and Bernie Sanders, you also possess something mighty and have everything you need to accomplish your purpose.

There are too many people creating excuses about not having enough time, not enough money, not enough education, not enough natural ability, not the right gender, not the right skin color, not old enough, not young enough, not in the right place, etc., for why they are unwilling to do something. They have everything physically needed for the task. What is lacking is the right attitude for the opportunity in front of them. The chains of unbelief, excuses, and idleness confine them to their current position.

What is that in your hand?

What do you currently possess?

What undervalued, underestimated, and marginalized resource(s) do you fail to make use of that, if fully utilized, could propel you to a position in life that you never imagined?

CHAPTER SUMMARY

Your Creator has seen fit to give you something of value according to your ability. It's what you do with what you are given that will determine whether you will receive more. Whether you have one talent, five, or ten, you will be held accountable for what you do with it. Don't spend time worrying about whether the talents you have are useful or whether the talents someone else has are better. Do not covet. Using the talent your Creator has given you should be your only thought and concern. If you do this to the best of your ability, you will have abundance.

You have unused talents and underutilized resources at your disposal right now. You are fully equipped to accomplish the task ahead of you. Perhaps you have allowed your current circumstance to cause you to forget former ideas, goals, and passions, and you find yourself now simply getting on with life. If this summarizes where you are, then it's time for you to stop making excuses, stop discounting the power within you, and to take the first step into your greatness. If you really want change, just do it and stop making excuses! If you do not like your current situation in life, be the source of your own rescue. Use your talents to take control of your future.

Part 2

The Path To Prosperity

You don't have to be like most people around you, because most people never become truly rich and wealthy. – Manoj Arora

The secret to making money isn't a high-paying job, it's finding creative solutions to people's problems. – Ziad K. Abdelnour

To have what you have never had, you have to do what you have never done. – Roy T. Bennett

5

DEDICATE YOURSELF TO LEARNING

Live as if you were to die tomorrow. Learn as if you were to live forever. – Mahatma Gandhi

The real asset of any advanced nation is its people, especially the educated ones, and the prosperity and success of the people are measured by the standards of their education. – Sheik Zayed, Founding Father of the UAE

Education is our passport to the future, for tomorrow belongs to the people who prepare for it today. – Malcolm X

This is one of several truths I have learned; man's greatest asset is his ability to think, learn, and educate himself. Education is the key to how you create, maintain, and expand your wealth as well as raise the standard of living for yourself and future generations.

To be honest, there are wealthy people that are not well educated, who have been able to achieve financial prosperity, perhaps capitalizing on their physical beauty, athletic prowess, or musical talent. These are the exception. The truth is, you have a better chance of being struck by lightning than becoming the next LeBron James or Beyoncé Knowles. For the majority of people on this planet, the quality and level of education they obtain often predict what type of job they will have and how much money they will earn.

Study the wealthiest countries and the most advanced societies in the world and you will see that one of the many things they have in common is good schools and a sound public education system.

The ability to provide quality education to its youth is the true strength of a nation. Indeed, an educated population is more important and sustainable than its natural resources such as oil wells, diamond mines, gold, fertile soil, and natural rain forests. Children are our greatest natural resource. Every progressive country that recognizes this will make a significant financial commitment to ensure that every child has free access to school and is able to receive a quality education.

As you advance further through this chapter, you will see that education has many intangible benefits, several things you may not have considered, that are worthy of discussion.

Education Is A Tool

Education makes life easier because it will raise your income potential and quality of life.

Education works as a tool.

Anyone that has ever tried to repair something – a car, a piece of furniture, or do handyman work – can appreciate having the right tool. While it's possible to repair many things with only a screwdriver, pliers, and a hammer, having the right tool for the job reduces the amount of time needed to make or repair something considerably. This is why people that engage in repair work or crafts spend a great deal of money on purchasing tools. They recognize that having the right tool brings efficiency – efficiency reduces the amount of time needed; the less time needed to complete a task lowers labor costs; lower labor costs increase profitability, and; higher profitability raises one's standard of living and quality of life.

They also recognize that the more tools they have, the more things they are able to repair.

Education works the same way. Education, like an extra tool on your tool belt, will make life easier by giving you the resources needed to solve problems. Education expands the type of work you are able to do, increases your income potential, and allows you to find solutions to problems more effectively. Education is the tool that never breaks and will not rust. Once it's obtained, unlike other finite resources, education can never be taken away.

A well-educated person is more flexible and better able to adapt to a changing environment. For example, a software developer must continue to learn new technologies to stay marketable. Staying up-to-date also creates additional employment and work from home opportunities. Many software developers freelance to earn extra money. In fact, many people have been able to become self-employed and earn their money working online by providing a needed service to global customers that are desperate for their technical skills.

If continuously learning new technologies sounds difficult, think of the alternative – their job skills will become obsolete and they risk becoming like the disgruntled automotive workers whose job have moved overseas. Even more troubling is, in the not too distant future, anyone whose job can be completed by a robot will soon be replaced. The world is moving rapidly into an age where the only jobs will be what robots can't do. This is bad news for truck drivers, insurance underwriters, tax preparers, low-level accountants, bookkeepers, bank tellers, loan officers, cashiers, textile workers, construction workers, and many other jobs that can be easily automated.

Beyond increasing your income opportunities, education also raises your self-esteem. An educated person has higher expectations, will not settle, will demand more, and will not be made to feel inferior. This is one of the primary reasons why southern states prohibited slaves from learning to read or attend school. They understood that education increases self-esteem – and with higher self-esteem brings empowerment, and with empowerment comes the desire for greater freedom.

Not to be forgotten, education can change a person's status and position in life. Few former slaves manifested this truth more than Frederick Douglass. Once a slave, Frederick Douglass learned how to read and became a famous orator and gifted writer, while also becoming a prominent social reformer and leader in the abolitionist movement.

An educated person will not remain a victim of circumstance and will use their education to find a way to improve their situation. In most cases, it's the uneducated along with people that discontinue learning that are easily manipulated and suffer the most in life.

EDUCATION IS A DEFENSE

Education is a tool but is also a defense system against those that seek to capitalize on your ignorance.

Sadly, profit has become the underlying motive that drives free market capitalism. While the desire for profit is not evil, the greed that is often present in a capitalistic system is. Greed, defined as *a selfish and excessive desire for something*, causes people to search diligently for ways to maximize profit, even if it means taking advantage of others to do it.

One of the ways a capitalist can benefit is by taking advantage of someone's ignorance and vulnerability. For example, if domestic laborers do not know that the going pay rate for cleaning services is $12 an hour, then there will be no shortage of employers who will pay them minimum wage, or less. This is a form of stealing that is not punishable by law. You can argue that this is not stealing because no one forced the employee to accept the job. However, paying someone less because they don't know any better, or because they are in a position where they cannot do any better, is immoral. Just because something is legal, doesn't make it right.

Good workers are entitled to a fair wage – to share the wealth they help produce. This fact is so important that it is written in the Bible in three separate texts and is found in both the Old and New Testament. It is best summarized in 1 Timothy 5:18, which says, "Those who work deserve their pay."

Whether a free market capitalist likes it or not, one cannot exist without the other. There is a symbiotic relationship between business owners and workers. Unless there is a well-paid, prosperous working class there will be very little prosperity for anyone because there will be few people that can afford to buy the goods produced by mass-markets and manufacturers.

There seems to be an endless number of millionaires that have made a fortune profiting from people's ignorance. Fast-talking salesmen have duped countless customers to purchase products they do not need by appealing to their emotions. An example is the used car salesman. They often utilize several tactics to deceive unsuspecting customers. Some of these include: clever wordplay; playing coy with pricing; extended loan terms; low-balling your trade-in; unnecessary upgrades and useless warranties; high financing rates; yo-yo financing – callbacks from the dealership after a few days saying that financing fell through and that to keep the vehicle, you'll have to settle for a higher interest rate or down payment, and; hiding the vehicle's history.

You don't have to fear a used car salesman or the buying process. Their Jedi mind tricks only work if you are ignorant. Arm yourself against their tactics by educating yourself about the buying process or the product you want to purchase.

You can ask someone for information if you lack knowledge, but I advise you to do your own research. Many people will freely give you anecdotal information that can lead you down the wrong path. Check multiple sources. Get the knowledge for yourself by reading. Take ownership of your own education. This is the only way you can be sure of the knowledge you receive.

Unfortunately, due to our natural inclination towards selfishness and greed – capitalism, over the long-term, is a zero-sum game. In order for someone to win, someone else has to lose.

For example, when a company reaches the maturity stage in its lifecycle one of the ways to increase market share is to develop a new product or service to attract new customers. This is very difficult to do. Therefore, senior management often pursues costs cutting measures to improve efficiency in order to increase profitability. Layoffs are typically the first action taken. However, when layoffs are not possible without hurting productivity, a capitalist must find someone willing to work for less.

Finding people that will work for less than the market rate is a race to the bottom. In most cases, if the labor force that is willing to accept less pay lives inside the country, they are generally not well educated or lack experience. Otherwise, they probably live in a country where wages are lower. It's for this reason why I firmly believe that the long-term outcome of capitalism is for rich people (typically those that are well educated) to find creative methods to separate poor people (the less educated) from their hard-earned money. Said differently, when it becomes too difficult for capitalists to make more money by becoming more efficient through innovation, they revert to cost-cutting by exploiting the uneducated. The only way to protect yourself from this form of exploitation is through education. Labor unions are simply not as powerful and relevant as they once were.

How does increasing one's education help to prevent exploitation?

For starters, education fosters the development of higher-order thinking skills – giving you the ability to recognize potential problems and figure out ways to solve them.

People that can solve complex problems are few in number. Therefore, higher-order thinking skills, achieved by a commitment to continue learning, will advance your status in life. If an entry-level employee can continuously demonstrate the capacity to solve complex problems, they will not remain in that position for very long. If their employer does not reward them for their problem-solving ability, another employer will. A competent employer will recognize an employee's ability to solve problems and promote them to a position of higher authority and added responsibility while increasing their pay.

COLLEGES AND UNIVERSITIES

Do a google search and you will see there is plenty of data and academic reports that show why education beyond secondary school is extremely important, especially if you want to increase your job opportunities and lifetime earnings. The U.S. Bureau of Labor Statistics has detailed data tables that show unemployment rates and earnings by educational attainment. These same reports will also show that education beyond the bachelor's degree will also increase your lifetime earnings beyond the typical college graduate.

Another differentiator in education and future earning potential is the school you attend. Each year, *U.S. News & World Reports* and other magazines publish revised college and university rankings. Students and parents use these rankings to determine the best schools to send admission applications. Companies seeking to attract summer interns and recent college graduates also use these rankings to decide which universities and colleges to schedule recruiting visits.

This is the first lesson I learned while pursuing tertiary education. Your academic success in high school, reflected by your grade point average (GPA), is an important factor in determining whether you are accepted into one of the top universities.

Secondly, students with low GPAs and poor academic performance in school leave money on the table and increase the cost of attending colleges and universities by not qualifying for academic scholarships and limiting their ability to negotiate a higher starting salary post-graduation. Either way, the outcome is the same because it results in lost money – the costs to attend school is not reduced and the potential for a higher starting salary is forfeited. GPA is an important factor in whether a person is selected for a coveted internship position. An internship can provide meaningful work experience and result in a full-time job offer if the work performed is satisfactory. For this reason, a company is often more willing to pay a higher starting salary for a person that has prior work experience.

With the rising cost of education and a competitive job market, few graduates can afford to limit their starting salary and career opportunities by producing noncompetitive grades.

TRADE SCHOOLS

The education that technical schools, also called trade schools, provide is no less important. The problem in the United States is there is a misguided belief that everyone, in order to obtain a good paying job, should attend a four-year university.

In many high schools across the country, technical classes have been removed. No longer are students able to take electives like woodshop, metals, automotive technology, barbering and the like. In order to prepare for a rigorous college curriculum, students are forced to take extra science and math classes. On the surface, this does not seem like a bad idea. Indeed, math and science learning are important. However, this assumes that the student has the desire and the ability to obtain a college degree. Unfortunately, this is not always the case. People are not all equipped with the same abilities and the proclivity to attend university. This does not mean that they should remain as unskilled laborers. On the contrary, they should have the opportunity and be encouraged to pursue a more technical path.

The dispersion of intellectual versus technical aptitude is what creates advanced societies. When society understands that not everyone is capable of doing the same task and that there must be a division of labor, the outcome is generally more positive. The unemployment rate is lower because each citizen has a chance to engage in a respectable line of work – which in turn allows them to earn a living wage and become a positive contributor to society.

Too often in America, students, not fit for university study, are encouraged to attend a four-year college program to pursue a degree that they will not complete. Had the student attended a shorter, two-year college and obtained desirable technical training, they would be more employable and able to enter the workforce sooner, and have less student loan debt, if any.

Some people will get uneasy whenever they hear of students being advised not to pursue a college degree and directed to pursue trade school instead. I recognize that many bright and capable students have been wrongly diverted away from attending college, when in fact, if they had attended, they would have been very successful. This is wrong. The point I want to make clear is, even if a student is directed to attend a trade school, after completing the coursework and obtaining their certificate, they will have obtained a marketable set of skills that will enable them to earn a living wage. In addition, there is nothing stopping the student from attending a public or private university later in life. The skill they acquired from trade school will not be lost.

For example, while it's common for many college students to hold a low paying part-time job in order to support themselves, a person with a desired technical skill can earn a higher wage and can often set their own work schedule.

Consider an experience I had in college. During my sophomore year, I would get my hair cut by a much older student that was a licensed barber. Instead of bussing tables at a restaurant where he would have been required to clock in and work on a schedule determined by someone else, he used his training to provide a needed service to students that desired a haircut and was able to set his own work hours. Students wanting a haircut would schedule appointments based on his schedule and availability. Because he was a licensed barber and not some random dude with clippers cutting hair in a dormitory bathroom, he was always fully booked. Moreover, he was paid in cash at the completion of his service and did not have to wait two weeks to receive a paycheck.

The point I want to make clear is this: all types of technical education obtained are useful – it can be utilized to save and make money. To save money, one can always use the acquired skill to repair their own car, service their air conditioner, and style their own or their family's hair, etc. The only limit to the numerous possibilities that a technical education can provide is your imagination.

EDUCATION THROUGH ENTREPRENEURSHIP

Apart from the knowledge and specialist training that a formal university or trade school can provide, there is a considerable amount of education and learning that is available through entrepreneurship. Not enough is not said regarding the merits of entrepreneurship.

If I were given a forum to address a large group of young people, I would choose a commencement ceremony at a college or university. I would tell this aspiring audience to pursue entrepreneurship on either a full-time or a part-time basis. For those graduates that will not be entering a Masters or Doctoral program and plan to enter the workforce, if they have the ability to do so, I would tell them – instead of seeking a job at a fortune 500 company – to start a business and go to work for yourself.

While entrepreneurship is beneficial and should be encouraged for all groups of people, there are few groups for which entrepreneurship is more needful than the African American community. As I will explain in later chapters, entrepreneurship is one of the best ways to build long-term capital. More importantly, entrepreneurship is the way forward to building a community that can thrive for generations to come.

STUDENT LOAN DEBT

With the staggering and rising costs of tuition and accompanying student loan debt that has overtaken the country, I understand the need to get a job quickly after graduation. The grace period before student loan payments are set to commence, at times, seems all too short and default must be avoided – as a breach of this nature can drastically damage your credit profile and even future job prospects, as well as harm your alma mater by leading to the elimination of the student loan program. Already, the student loan default rate at many colleges and universities is disproportionality high, causing considerable angst and stress for school administrators who struggle to find ways to secure funding so that the institution's doors can remain open. For many ambitious students, loans are the primary source of funding available and the only thing that makes the realization of a college degree possible.

Sadly, far too many students find themselves encumbered with high student loan debt and limited job prospects after graduation. After spending four years pursuing what later seems to be a worthless degree – and let me suggest that many college majors do not adequately prepare students to enter the workforce, the graduate soon realizes that they have lost considerable time and money. Unfortunately, the time spent to obtain a degree is unrecoverable but the student loans remain and require repayment. This is a travesty and failure of the government and educational system.

Unfortunately, even though the percentage of African American and Hispanic students attending college is lower than white students, and the percentage of those that actually graduate with a degree in four years is even lower, African American college graduates are the undisputed champions holding the title as the largest percentage of educated job seekers having difficulty finding work within their field of study.

Let me be clear, I do not suggest that a four-year college degree is unimportant or a waste of time and money. Rather, for some, I believe it makes sense to delay the pursuit of a four-year degree until they better understand future job prospects and know what field they want to work in.

There are literally thousands of colleges and universities in the United States seeking domestic and international students. A few may disappear due to poor management and insolvency, but those that remain will be more than happy to accept your admissions application and tuition money at a later time.

CONTINUE TO READ

Everyone should make a commitment to continue learning. One of the best ways to do this is through reading. Therefore, find time to read. Make time if you have to. If you make time to read, I guarantee that you will notice several favorable changes. Your knowledge, awareness, critical thinking skills, and ability to communicate will improve. This will have a positive effect on your life.

Make reading fun. If you do not like to read, maybe it's because you haven't found books that interest you. You don't have to read only one category of books. Mix them up. Book clubs are a great way to discover different types of books to read. There are several different genres for you to choose from; they are as diverse as the colors you see on birds. The various categories include: arts and photography, biographies, business, cooking, history, mystery and suspense, religion, romance, and science fiction, to name just a few.

Read to become educated. I know several people that do not have a college degree but are some of the most educated in the world. They can have an intelligent conversation, providing facts, statistics, historical context, across several topics with relative ease. There are few subjects where they are completely ignorant. In fact, you would never know that they did not have a college degree unless they told you. Alternatively, I know several "educated" people that hold advanced degrees but are some of the most ignorant people to walk the planet. They are narrow-minded, uninformed, simple, and easily influenced. They proudly project rhetoric that is void of facts and basic common sense. They are not well read; they stopped reading the moment they graduated college or, if they do read, their scope is too narrow to be of any benefit.

Don't make the mistake of believing that the amount of schooling one has is a reflection of their education. It was Mark Twain who said, "I never allowed my schooling to get in the way of my education."

Read to avoid making mistakes. The Bible says, "My people are destroyed for lack of knowledge" (Hosea 4:6). In a high-speed world where free information, on just about every topic, is available at our fingertips, there is no excuse for making stupid mistakes because of lack of knowledge. If you lack knowledge in a certain area or want to find out more about a subject, do a google search, go to a library, borrow a book, buy a book, but whatever you do – read! Don't use the excuse, "No one ever told me" for making avoidable mistakes.

CHAPTER SUMMARY

Education has an immense value that is far greater than any finite natural resource found in the ground. The ability of a people to educate themselves and their offspring is the true measure of the wealth of a nation. Education has a monetary value that no human being can measure. But, not only does it have monetary value, it also offers other intrinsic attributes that are necessary for a high quality of life. Education has two real-life functions: 1) it's a tool to make life easier and, 2) it's a defense system to keep you from being exploited.

A formal education can be obtained by attending a college or university program or attending a trade school. A sound argument can be made for choosing one over the other. Regardless of the learning path chosen, the benefits that come from school is never lost. Whether the derived benefit is higher-order thinking skills or learning a specific trade, these attributes will help to raise your income and quality of life.

Learning should never be limited to only a formal education program. Each person should make a commitment to life-long learning by reading. Expand your mind, knowledge, understanding, vocabulary, and awareness of the world by reading. You don't need a college degree in order to be "educated." Likewise, having a college degree alone does not make you "educated."

6

THINK BIG

Not failure, but low aim is sin. – Benjamin Elijah Mays

Your words control your life, your progress, your thoughts, even your mental and physical health. You cannot talk like a failure and expect to be successful. – Germany Kent

It costs nothing to think bigger than you are, BUT cost a fortune to think less of yourself. – Olawale Daniel

There is a sin of not thinking big. Benjamin Elijah Mays, an American Baptist minister, civil rights activists, humanitarian, educator, and former president of Morehouse College uttered these very powerful words:

"It must be borne in mind that the tragedy of life doesn't lie in not reaching your goal. The tragedy lies in having no goal to reach. It isn't a calamity to die with dreams unfulfilled, but it is a calamity not to dream. It is not a disaster to be unable to capture your ideal, but it is a disaster to have no ideal to capture. It is not a disgrace not to reach the stars, but it is a disgrace to have no stars to reach for. Not failure, but low aim is sin."

I once heard a wise man tell his children, "I won't have a problem if you aim high and miss, but I'm going to have a real issue with you if you aim low and hit."

DESIRE

The desire to want more is not sinful. Actually, it's a God-like trait. God desired more and created the heavens and the earth; and the Creator gave you a similar desire, the desire to yearn for more. God instructed Adam and Eve to, "Be fruitful and multiply. Fill the earth and govern it" (Genesis 1:28). This means that man was supposed to increase in population and not stay in one place. We were supposed to branch out and fill the entire earth. In order for that to occur, someone had to reject the status quo and exercise their internal desire to move away from the familiar and explore the unknown. Desire was a necessary emotion needed to propel us forward, forcing our thoughts to become physical actions.

God put within you a natural impulse to want more. Your Creator also gave you the intelligence to enlarge yourself and a longing to extend your boundaries and find fuller expression of your inner desires. The manifestation of your intelligence and consciousness is brought to life through your thoughts and well-defined words.

THE POWER OF THOUGHTS

For many people, the problem is not that they lack desire; it's that they have lost the ability to convert their thoughts into action. They have repressed their God-given ability and right to "subdue" creation, or take action, because they have lost the power to control their mind.

Let me explain this further by using a short story.

There is a story about an old Native American man teaching his grandson about life.

"A fight is going on inside of me", he said to the boy. "It is a terrible fight and it is between two wolves. One is evil – he is anger, envy, sorrow, regret, greed, arrogance, self-pity, guilt, resentment, inferiority, lies, false pride, superiority, and ego."

He continued.

"The other is good – he is joy, peace, love, hope, serenity, humility, kindness, benevolence, empathy, generosity, truth, compassion, and faith. The same fight is going on inside of you – and inside of every other person."

The grandson thought about it for a minute and then asked his grandfather, "Which wolf will win?"

The old Cherokee simply replied, "The one you feed."

The lesson from this is to be very careful which thoughts you feed.

Thoughts spring from your mind and have immense power when they are put into action. Your thoughts become ideas, and ideas, when acted upon, have the power to transform and shape the natural world. Man can form things in his thoughts. All the forms that man fashions with his hands must first exist in his thoughts; he cannot shape a thing until he has thought that thing in his mind. We can then conclude that thoughts are the precursor of activity.

To transform something is to overpower it by force, to bring it under physical, mental, or emotional control. Because of the overpowering nature of sin, controlling our thoughts is more difficult. In Romans 12:2 Paul says,

"Be a new and different person with a fresh newness in all you do and think. Then you will learn from your own experience how his ways will really satisfy you."

In other words, subdue your thoughts by renewing your mind. When your thoughts are subdued and in alignment with God's perfect will, Jesus promised, "You may ask anything in my name, and I will do it" (John 14:14). Your desire must be linked and in alignment with God's perfect will.

The question then becomes, what is God's perfect will and how do I know God's will for my life?

Jeremiah 29:11 says, "For I know the plans I have for you...plans for good and not for disaster, to give you a future and a hope." God's plans for you extend beyond this earth. His desire is for you to be included in his kingdom when he returns. In order for that to occur, you must live a righteous life on earth, and as Jesus said to his disciples "occupy till I come." Righteous living means following God's commandments. Jesus said, "If you love me, keep my commandments" (John 14:15). His commandments are summarized into two love commandments – "You must love the Lord your God will all your heart, all your soul, and all your mind...Love your neighbor as yourself" (Matthew 22:37-39). Very simply, God's will for your life is that you live a life of righteousness exemplified by following his commandments and demonstrated by acts of service towards your fellow man.

A life of service is God's desire for your life and we are to follow his example – "I have given you an example to follow. Do as I have done to you" (John 13:15). Following Christ's example is His will for you. A life dedicated to service is – raising the standard of living and quality of life of those around you and improving the world you live in through kindness and charity. This should be your highest goal. When you live a life of service you are in God's perfect will; your thoughts and desires become one with His. When this occurs, you can ask *anything* in his name and it will be granted. This includes resources that you can use to bless others that are less fortunate.

A life of service does not necessarily require money, but it does require time. However, in order to bless as many people as possible in your neighborhood, city, or around the world requires that you have money or access to resources. Therefore, you must get rid of the notion that it is God's desire that you remain poor, or that your living in poverty somehow serves His purpose. This is simply not true. His desire is that you make the most of yourself, for yourself, so that you can help others; you can help others more by becoming rich or gaining access to resources. The Bible says the sick and poor will always be among us, but it does not say that you have to be one of them.

Your situation in life is not predetermined.

Your beginning does not determine your end.

GUARD YOUR THOUGHTS

Published in 2000, *The Prayer of Jabez: Breaking Through to the Blessed Life*, became a best-seller, topping the New York Times bestseller list. The underlying message that is the central theme of the Jabez prayer is undeniable. Jabez wanted more. He was not satisfied with the status quo. Indeed, desire for more is at the heart of Jabez's prayer.

When your thoughts and desires are aligned with God's, there is no room for negative thinking. Jabez had every reason to have a negative outlook on life. His mother named him Jabez, which means "he causes pain" in Hebrew. Despite this unfortunate name choice, Jabez did not allow this to control his thinking. No matter how he was perceived and what others thought of him, he was unwilling to settle. He wanted more from life and asked God to expand his territory.

Jabez did not think of himself as a victim of circumstance, he saw favor. When he took inventory of his life he did not see poverty, he saw abundance. This mindset is required if you ever desire wealth. You must train your mind to shun appearances when it is contrary to truth. To think confidently of future prosperity when in the midst of the appearances of poverty is difficult and requires the power of a focused mind.

Things are not brought into this world by thinking about their opposites. Life is not created by thinking about death; righteousness is not promoted by thinking about sin, and; no one gets rich by studying poverty.

I doubt many people fully understand the destructive nature of negative thinking. Countless people have allowed negative thinking and people's perception of them to adversely affect their outlook on life and ability to look beyond their current situation. Because of negative perceptions about their race, gender, nationality, socioeconomic status, and family background, many people have unknowingly become their own worst enemy and have allowed negative thinking to rob them of a better future. Negative thinking can affect every area of your life and keep you from pursuing the things you really want. Negative thinking can make you tell yourself, "I'm never going to go to college. I'm never going to get that job. I'm never going to get married. I'm never going to be debt free. I'm never going to lose weight." Even worse, negative thinking will make you believe it.

Stop filling your mind with negative thoughts!

The Bible warns us against negative thinking.

Philippians 4:8 says,

"Fix your thoughts on what is true, and honorable, and right, and pure, and lovely, and admirable. Think about things that are excellent and worthy of praise."

In this text, Paul admonishes you to fill your mind with only positive thoughts, regardless of your situation. Paul understood the power of positive thinking.

Paul was very familiar with adversity and had to overcome some very challenging situations. Three times he was beaten, he was stoned, and he was shipwreck three times spending one day and night in the open sea (2 Corinthians 11:25). Paul could have allowed these trials and tribulations to overcome him, losing all hope for survival by focusing on his present circumstance. He could have allowed negative thoughts to defeat him. Instead of focusing on the bad, Paul subdued his thoughts with positive thinking.

In a survival situation, your thoughts can determine whether you will live or die. If you tell yourself you are going to die, you dramatically increase the odds that you will. However, if you tell yourself that you will live you increase the odds of your survival.

Positive thinking was the key to God answering Jabez's prayer of expansion. Positive thinking is the way to change your financial position in life and the life of others. If you want to escape poverty, you have to remove pictures of poverty from your mind first. If you want to reduce poverty in the world, start by putting pictures of wealth into the minds of the poor. The world doesn't need more charitable people that think about poverty, it needs more poor people who purpose in their heart, with faith, a goal to become wealthy. Not everyone that is poor needs charity; many times what they need is inspiration and an opportunity. If you want to help as many poor people as possible, prove to them that they can become wealthy by becoming wealthy yourself. Become a living example that someone like yourself can become rich. This is the best way you can help the poor.

THE POWER OF WORDS

Many people underestimate the power of speech – thinking that it only represents a form of verbal expression. If this is your belief, you are wrong. Words are so much more than that. Words are not just sounds uttered from your mouth. Words have power over the physical realm, bringing into existence that which was not there before or altering the course of something already present by reducing it to nothing. This was a power given to mankind by our Creator.

When our Creator decided to bring our world into existence, He spoke these words in Genesis 1, "Let there be", and over the course of six days, the world was formed. Light was divided from the darkness. The sky was separated from the water below. Dry land was formed along with grass, plants, and trees. The stars, sun, and the moon were created. Fish and all other living things in the sea were created. On the sixth day, our Creator caused every living creature that moves upon the earth and dry land to come into existence. These things were brought forth by our Creator's spoken words. Then God said,

> "Let us make human beings in our image, to be like us. They will reign over the fish of the sea, the birds in the sky, the

livestock, all the wild animals on the earth, and the small animals that scurry along the ground" (Genesis 1:26).

When our Creator brought mankind into existence he did something more, something greater. Mankind was not *spoken* into existence, we were *formed* using dust from the ground and fashioned into God's very own image and after His likeness. Then our Creator did something truly powerful and awesome. Unlike the animals and every other living beast created, our Creator knelt down over the first man's lifeless body and breathed into his nostrils the breath of life, and the man became a living person. Our Creator breathed *Himself* – his essence, his power, into us. I doubt many people are able to grasp what this really means.

Our Creator spoke words to exercise His power over the earth, and it was so. When God gave mankind dominion over this planet, we were given similar power and authority. Our voice can cause a whale to jump into the air, an elephant to kneel, and birds to take flight. Our power is not limited to this only. With our spoken words, we can exercise dominion over all the earth – everything physical. Jesus said, "If you have the faith as a grain of mustard seed, you will say to this mountain, 'Move from here to there', and it will move; and nothing will be impossible for you" (Matthew 17:20). And because our Creator breathed into us part of himself, you also possess the power to speak what you desire into existence – not instantly, but in the process of time. Like our Creator, your ability to create starts with an internal desire, a thought, spoken words, and necessary action.

Atheists have worked diligently to remove God from creation by focusing on science alone. In so doing, they unknowingly limit human potential by denying who we *really* are, children of the Most High God, and what we are capable of; thereby, denying mankind's power to exercise dominion over the physical world simply by our thoughts and words.

GUARD YOUR WORDS

Spoken words yield incredible power. Words have the power to create and destroy. Words have the power to build up and tear down. The Bible tells us that blessings and curses are in the power of the tongue. Therefore, chose your words carefully. Be careful of what you say. Never speak words of negativity upon yourself. Reject all negative remarks and opinions spoken by others, especially if it has anything to do with your future and the goals you have set for yourself. Remove "I can't" from your vocabulary. Stop limiting yourself by thinking and speaking failure into your life.

Some of the greatest innovators, artist, leaders, and businessmen this world has seen refused to accept no as an answer for themselves, or from someone else. Consider four individuals: Bill Gates, Stephen King, Abraham Lincoln, and Jack Ma.

Bill Gates is famous for being one of the richest men in the world. Before launching Microsoft, he and fellow partner Paul Allen created a company that failed. Bill Gates could have given up on his dream, but instead, he used the lessons learned from failing to create Microsoft. The Microsoft Windows logo is recognized on every continent in the world and the software is present in every computer that is not a Mac.

Stephen King is one of the most successful novelists of our time. However, before he became a renowned writer, he was a high school English teacher who could not get his novels published. In fact, his first published novel, *Carrie*, was rejected by numerous publishers before being accepted. Rejection could have destroyed Stephen King and he could have gone on being an English teacher struggling to make ends meet. But he kept pushing forward. Now, Stephen King is a household name having sold over 350 million copies of his books, many of which have been made into movies, miniseries, television shows, and comic books.

Abraham Lincoln is considered by many to be one of the United States' greatest Presidents. As the sixteenth President, he led the country through one of its most difficult periods – the Civil War. But before he became President, his career was marred by many failures. In 1832, at age 23, Lincoln, along with his partner, owned a small general store in New Salem, Illinois. Despite the booming economy in the region, the business was unsuccessful and Lincoln sold his share. It was in March of the same year that he began his political career. He was not an immediate success. Eight times Lincoln ran for public office and lost. It took 28 years before he would become President of the United States.

Jack Ma is one of the world's most successful entrepreneurs. However, before he founded Alibaba and became the richest man in China, Ma failed in almost all of his endeavors. In fact, he failed more times than most people could bare in a lifetime.

Here are just a few of the notable ways that Ma experienced failure.

1. Ma was a poor math student. He was so bad at math that he scored a 1 out of 120 points on the math portion of his college entrance exam.
2. He was rejected by Harvard University 10 times.

3. After graduating from college, he applied to 30 different jobs and was rejected by all of them.
4. Out of 24 applicants, Ma was the only one rejected by Kentucky Fried Chicken (KFC).
5. Even after he started Alibaba, he couldn't convince Silicon Valley to fund his company. Alibaba wasn't profitable for the first three years. In fact, it almost failed.
6. Ma made one of the worst decisions a CEO can make. Ma told 18 partners that none of them could rise higher than the position of manager. He wanted to hire outside directors instead.

Despite his numerous, gut-wrenching failures, Ma did not let this crush his spirit; he managed to keep his optimism. He didn't give up on pursuing his dreams.

BELIEVE

Before anyone sets out to accomplish something, they have never done before, if they desire to be successful, they must first believe that they can actually do it. The outcome is enhanced by believing versus doubting. Your mindset is a strong predictor of whether you will obtain your goal. Your success and achievement in life are proportionate to your belief and your level of perseverance. You cannot quit. You have to keep pushing forward and believe in yourself.

Jesus said, "Anything is possible for someone that has faith" (Mark 9:2).

Does this mean that people that believe in themselves will always achieve everything they desire?

No.

The text does not say *it will always happen*; it says anything is *possible*.

Having said that, there are times when a man must embrace his limitations and draw power from a supernatural force if something is to be obtained. While prayer is no shortcut for what others must work for, and it is always necessary to put forth maximum effort as though success depends on you alone, there will be times when you will need to ask help from your Father to avoid failure. Jesus said, "With men this is impossible, but with God all things are possible" (Matthew 19:26).

More things are obtained by prayer than this world will ever fully know. There are certain blessings and outcomes that you will never receive unless you ask for them; they are granted by request only. James 4:2 says, "You have not because you ask not."

If you ask, ask in faith.

"But let him ask in faith, with no doubting" (James 1:6). The verse goes on by comparing a man that doubts to waves in the sea tossed by the wind. James calls anyone that comes to God with a request double-minded and unstable if they are doubtful as to whether it will be granted. But more important than this strong reprimand is the fact that they should not expect to receive anything from the Lord.

The willingness of God to grant your requests is nullified by unbelief. The sixth chapter of Mark illustrates this fact.

Jesus visits his home country with his disciples. On the Sabbath, Jesus entered a synagogue and began to teach. Instead of the town's inhabitants accepting him with warmth they were offended and challenged his authority. Despite their awareness of the miracles Jesus had performed outside the region, he was just too familiar and they didn't respect him. They remembered him as a carpenter. They knew his brothers: James, Joses, Judas, and Simon, and his sisters still lived in the area. Jesus said to them, "A prophet is not without honor except in his own country, among his own relatives, and in his own house." What verse 58 states is astonishing. It says, "Now He could do no mighty work there, except He laid His hands on a few sick people and healed them."

Jesus performed incredible miracles and healed everyone that came to him. However, in his home country, all he could do was heal a few sick people. This was because of their unbelief. If you want to receive above average, supernatural results, come to your Maker with your requests. But, before you come, leave your unbelief behind.

CHAPTER SUMMARY

When your thoughts and words are aligned with focused, consistent, unwavering belief in yourself, and is backed with action, there are few things you cannot accomplish. Our Creator has made this so by giving mankind His own power to transform the physical world with our words, for we were formed in His image and in His likeness. This ability was a gift to all, believer and unbeliever alike. That is why atheists can be successful at accumulating riches and great wealth, even though they have no respect for God and deny He is their creator. Speaking of the Father, Jesus said, "For He makes His sun rise on the evil and on the good, and sends rain on the just and on the unjust" (Matthew 5:45). The same sentiment was voiced by one of Jesus' disciples, Peter, when he said, "Of a truth I perceive that God is no respecter of persons" (Acts 10:34).

There is a hidden science, a natural law, behind the power of directed thoughts and spoken words. You would be wise to respect this law as much as you respect the law of gravity. You wouldn't dare jump off a 100-story building without a net to catch you. This would be incredibly stupid. Similarly, it's foolish to think and speak words of negativity upon yourself as this can be equally as dangerous, causing injury from which you may never recover. Few have achieved greatness by telling themselves something is impossible whereas millions of underachievers have embraced the words "I can't."

There are limits to your capabilities. As such, there are occasions when supernatural influence is needed. A wise man will recognize this and seek help from his Creator. There are some things that will only be granted by request. Even our earthly parents will not give us certain things unless we specifically ask for them. When you ask, believe that you will receive it. God will not be mocked.

7

FIND YOUR MONEY TREE

I always knew I was going to be rich. I don't think I ever doubted it for a minute. –
Warren Buffet

Rich people do not work for money, but work passionately until the end of their lives. –
Sunday Adelaja

Opportunities just don't happen. You create them. – Hyacil Han

There is no shortage of business opportunities (money trees) available from which you can become rich. Indeed, it seems that money is just lying around waiting for individuals who are ready to seize it. Money doesn't discriminate; it doesn't care or have any regard for race, nationality, gender, age, religion, or creed; it only looks for the person that is willing to seize the opportunity and is willing to do things in a particular way. Membership in the Millionaire's Club is growing exponentially all over the world and there is plenty of room for those who are willing to join by embracing a progressive, non-defeatist, and hard-working mindset. The world is thirsty for young professionals who are willing to become the next generation of innovators, entrepreneurs, and business leaders – instead of those that listen to naysayers, complaining that all the good ideas and opportunities have been taken.

No path to riches is so difficult that only a few can follow it. If this were the case, the world would have few rich people. But this is not the case. Many people are rich. Amongst the rich are the well-educated, uneducated, talented, untalented, physically strong, and disabled. There is no single factor that determines whether someone can become rich.

Getting rich is also not restricted to a specific location for there are people that have become rich in every location around the world. However, location does count in some ways. There must be some degree of population density. One would not go to a sparsely populated region and expect to be successful in business or commerce. There must be enough people to create demand.

No one is kept from getting rich because of lack of capital. Some people will say, and many believe, that it takes money to make money. As long as you have the capacity to think and generate ideas, you have capital of an intellectual kind. There are times when you may have more time than money. Leisure time should be spent on creativity and developing good ideas. Ideas do not require capital. Acting on ideas requires time. It's the poor use of time that truly makes one poor. Show me someone that is poor in managing their time and I will show you someone heading down the road to poverty. If you have a good idea and a well-planned way to follow through on your idea, the capital to fund your idea will invariably come.

If you have no capital, actively look for ways to get capital. If you are in the wrong business, get into the right business. If you are in the wrong location, move to the right location. No one is kept poor because an opportunity has been permanently taken away from them or because a person or some group of people have cornered the wealth or placed a barrier around it. No one is kept in poverty by a deficiency in the supply of money; there is more than enough for the man that actively seeks it and who is unwilling to stop until he obtains it.

You may be blocked from engaging in a certain line of business or profession, but there are other channels open to you. Opportunity comes from recognizing problems and developing a solution to solve them. Find a problem that affects numerous people, or a common need, and work to find a solution and you will become rich. Even better, find a way to produce something faster or at a cheaper cost. The road to riches starts with one good idea from which everyone can benefit.

Many times, acting on a good idea requires change. Changing your circumstance begins by making the most of your present vocation, often in your present location, by choosing to do things in a *particular way*. There is an abundance of opportunity for the man who will swim with the tide, instead of trying to fight against the current.

Do you live in a poor, undeveloped community that has fertile soil, a year-round growing season, and generous rainfall?

Start an agri-business by growing high-value crops for local consumption or export on land that is available.

Do you live in a community where the economy is contracting and the population is aging?

Start a business catering to the many needs of senior citizens by providing in-home (non-medical) services, money management and financial planning, tailoring services, fix-it services, home delivery services, lawn care and maintenance, computer consulting, nutrition and fitness consulting, etc.

The world is established in such a manner that the wind of opportunity blows in different directions according to mankind's needs at the time. However, ideas require action before any success can be achieved. An idea without action is like a car without wheels – it won't take you anywhere.

Becoming rich is not a matter of choosing one particular business or profession over another. There are people becoming rich in every business and in every profession, while others in the same vocation continue to struggle. Becoming rich does require doing things in a *particular way*.

Doing things in a *particular way* does generally require that you pursue a business or vocation in something you enjoy. It will be very difficult to become rich doing something that you detest or something for which you have very little interest. If you have certain talents, which are aptly developed, you will do best in a business that uses those talents.

Also, you will do best in a business that is suited to your current location. You won't be very successful selling air conditioners in cold climates when what is really needed is a good heating system.

If you study people that have become wealthy, you will find that the vast majority of them have no greater physical talents or mental abilities than others. They do not become rich because they possess talents and abilities that others do not have. They do not get rich by doing things that others fail to do; for two men in the same line of work or business often do almost exactly the same things, and one becomes successful and rich while the other does not.

To get rich, you must do things in a *particular way*.

Model the behavior and best practices of successful people and businesses. While no one can offer a precise formula or guarantee 100% success in any business, there are ten fundamental rules that tip the odds of success in your favor, if they are followed. These rules have worked for several self-made millionaires and they will work for you, too.

1. Own your own business. Almost without exception, most millionaires will tell you that owning your own business is the best way to make a large amount of money in the business world.

2. Never lose the central aim of all business – to produce more and better goods or to provide more and better services to more people at a lower cost.

3. Always practice thrift. Develop an eye for how to cut costs. This is essential in your personal life as well as business.

4. Never overlook legitimate opportunities for expansion. Grow your business by taking thoughtful, measured steps. Forced growth, or growing too quickly, can often end in ruin.

5. Mind your own business. Be careful of delegating too much authority to hired business managers. Always maintain close and constant supervision over staff, without fail.

6. Never become complacent. The business owner should always be alert for ways to improve their products or services to increase production and sales.

7. Be willing to take risks. When the risk is justified – when the potential reward outweighs the chance of failure – be willing to risk your own capital and borrowed money. "Nothing ventured, nothing gained" is one of the tenants of doing business.

8. Expand your market. The market has become global. There are emerging markets and a rising middle-

class anxious to purchase desired products and services. The businessman should actively look for ways to reach these untapped markets.

9. Always stand behind your work or product. Don't sell or offer any product or service that you would be unwilling to purchase or use yourself. Honor all guarantees and service agreements – and in the few doubtful cases, the decision should always be in the customer's favor. Develop a good name for reliability and you will have little trouble getting repeat business and customer referrals.

10. Never forget the purpose of why a business operates. A business must never lose sight of the fact that it operates so that its products and services can improve life and living conditions everywhere. After a reasonable profit is made, a portion of the business's accumulated wealth should be returned to its employees, investors, and the overall community.

Can getting rich really be this easy?

The answer is yes, when you do things in a *particular way* – knowing that getting rich seldom involves working the typical hours found in a standard nine-to-five job. In almost every circumstance, the secret to success boils down to being willing to do what others are not.

Possessing The Money Tree Attitude

A big part of doing things in a *particular way* starts with thinking in a *particular way* – having the money tree attitude. A tree has the potential to bear fruit each year as long as its roots are embedded in a solid foundation and the tree is properly nourished. Your mind is a tree that can bear numerous thoughts – fruit. Therefore, make sure that your mind has a deep root system that is nourished by positive thinking. Do not allow doubt or negative thinking to corrupt your root system from reaching deep into the soil of opportunity.

Once you have identified your business opportunity – your specific type of money tree – you must never allow yourself to think in a negative manner. You must never think that the supply of something is limited. Do not allow yourself to think that someone can prevent you from getting what is rightfully yours. Never think that you will lose what you desire because someone else has beat you to it or stolen your opportunity. Eliminate negative thinking from your mind and lose any spirit of fear. Prune off the negative branches that will prevent the good branches from growing fruit.

You must denounce the idea of scarcity. There is enough for everyone; you do not have to take away something from someone else. You are to create opportunities from the raw materials that God has given you and from what already exists. By becoming a creator, not a competitor, you summon the divine spirit within you to get what you want, but in such a manner that when you get it others will benefit as well.

You will not have to cheat or take advantage of someone else. You will not have to treat them unfairly. You will not have to try to get something for nothing. You do not need to allow any man to do more work for less than he earns. Instead, you can give to every man more than you take from him in labor. If you have someone working for you, never take more in labor than what you can give them through advancement, so that each employee who desires to do so may advance a little each day.

Another part of having a money tree attitude is handling adversity. Unfortunate things happen in life. Try as you might to avoid them, sometimes bad things happen anyway. What matters most is how you respond in these situations.

Do not lose your composure.

Do not give up.

Do not fall into a pit of negativity.

A money tree attitude requires that you accept life's misfortunes thoughtfully – taking them in stride, not allowing yourself to get discouraged for too long. Instead, use each setback to help motivate you to try again, using more effort to make sure that you succeed. Sometimes failure can be a foundation on which you can build.

PLANT A LARGE TREE

There are different types of fruit trees and they can come in different sizes. There are dwarf trees, semi-dwarf trees, and standard trees.

Dwarf fruit trees will grow 8 to 10 feet tall and wide, and depending on the environment, generally, start bearing fruit sooner than semi-dwarf and standard trees. Dwarf trees can be grown in containers and are ideal for places where space is limited.

Semi-dwarf is the next largest size of fruit trees. These trees reach 12 to 15 feet in height and have a similar width. They also yield more fruit. The average semi-dwarf tree may yield almost twice as much fruit as a dwarf-size tree, without taking up much more space. With proper care and pruning, they can grow comfortably in containers, although a garden or small yard is preferred.

A standard tree is the largest sized tree of any variety. When a standard tree has grown to its full mature size, these fruit trees can reach 18 to 25 plus feet in height and width. Standard trees may take longer to bear fruit, but once they get started, they will produce a greater volume of fruit than dwarf and semi-dwarf trees. At maturity, these trees may require the use of a ladder or a fruit picker to help you harvest the fruit. The yield will be so much that it will be more than you can eat by yourself.

When planning and selecting your money tree idea, don't limit yourself to only dwarf or semi-dwarf trees. Think big, not small. Don't choose any type of business opportunity that once it reaches its maximum size and maturity can fit nicely in a container. Why limit yourself this way?

Don't go into any business opportunity with the intent of only planting small trees. God is a giver, and His desire is for you to have abundance, to be used for your own enjoyment and to share with others. Start small, but position yourself in such a manner that you can plant the largest tree possible of one type of tree in order to obtain the largest yield.

Don't try to diversify by planting several different species of trees. This is a mistake often made by people immature in the ways of business. They split their attention by trying to do too much of everything, becoming a jack-of-all-trades, and end up becoming a master of nothing. They would do better by concentrating their efforts in one area, doing only one thing, learning as much as there is to know about that one thing as possible. Think and work like a skilled arborist; be meticulous in your cultivation by learning to pay attention to even the smallest details.

Be Thankful For Your Harvest

When your money tree produces a bountiful harvest, do not allow yourself to become overly conceited. Remember that God gave you the ability to create wealth (Deuteronomy 8:18). Yes, your mind may have created the thought, and your hands responded to the desire, and your hard work and labor may have prepared you for the opportunity, but God is the source from which all things proceed. Therefore, you should always have a feeling of deep gratitude for your success. An attitude of gratitude brings you into closer contact and communion with your Creator. Moreover, He appreciates your thankfulness. Allow me to illustrate this fact with a passage in Luke 17:11-18.

> As Jesus continued on toward Jerusalem, he reached the border between Galilee and Samaria. As he entered a village there, ten men with leprosy stood at a distance, crying out, "Jesus, Master, have mercy on us!" He looked at them and said, "Go show yourself to the priests." And as they went, they were cleansed of their leprosy. One of them, when he saw that he was healed, came back to Jesus, shouting, "Praise God!" He fell to the ground at Jesus' feet, thanking him for what he had done. This man was a Samaritan. Jesus asked, "Didn't I heal ten men? Where are the nine? Has no one returned to give glory to God except for this foreigner?"

The ten men that approached Jesus for healing correctly recognized that he could help them. They knew that if they were to be healed they needed a power greater than themselves. However, after becoming healed, nine of them quickly forgot about Jesus – too busy enjoying their current situation to utter a word of thanks. Shamefully, a Samaritan was the only one of the ten men that came near to Jesus (for previously they stood at a distance), falling down at his feet, to say thank you. His attitude

108

of gratitude and act of thanksgiving is what brought him closer to Jesus.

It should not be a surprise to know that the soul that expresses gratitude for their blessings lives in closer contact with God than someone that never draws closer to Him in thankful appreciation. "Draw nigh to God, and he will draw nigh to you" (James 4:8). If your gratitude is strong and consistent, God stands ready to hear the additional desires of your heart. Remember the grateful attitude and manner in which Jesus spoke, the number of times that he said to the Father, "I thank thee." Our gratitude is what keeps us connected to God, the source of our power.

There is a Law of Gratitude and it is absolutely necessary that you observe this law. Non-observance will disconnect you from your source of strength. Like the nine lepers that did not return, they sever the vines that connect them to the tree of life by failing to offer thanks.

There is a saying, "When praises go up the blessings come down." In Psalms 67, God tells his people to praise him.

Praise God always.

Praise God continually.

Let everything that has breath praise the Lord.

CHAPTER SUMMARY

Make every effort to find your money tree by investigating the opportunities around you. Start by identifying problems and devising a plan to solve them. No one is prevented from getting rich because of lack of opportunity or capital. Think of creative ways to solve as many problems as possible. If your ideas are good, the capital needed to implement your ideas will eventually come.

If you conduct yourself in a *particular way*, there will be no shortages of opportunities or ways to pursue commerce. There is more than enough money for the man that actively seeks it. If you have certain talents, which are aptly developed, you will do best in a business that uses those talents. Make changes when necessary. Model the behavior and practices of successful people. Learn to flow with the tide of opportunity instead of fighting against the current. You won't be successful in making money by doing the opposite of what is needed.

Develop the right attitude for success by staying positive. You must not allow negative thinking to cloud your mind. Your money tree will never bear fruit if it is nourished with the fertilizer of negative thinking.

Always recognize God as the source of your strength and remember to thank Him whenever your ventures are successful.

8

TRADING TIME FOR DOLLARS

Time management is the major difference between the rich and the poor. – Sunday Adelaja

Every day is a bank account, and time is our currency. No one is rich, no one is poor, we've got 24 hours each. – Christopher Rice

Time is a currency you can only spend once, so be careful how you spend it. – Harmon Okinyo

If you desire to earn a high income, there are many career paths available for you to choose in just about every industry and business sector. You can become a doctor, engineer, computer programmer, lawyer, management consultant, investment banker, corporate executive, pilot, etc. All these professions pay high wages relative to the average income but often require education beyond the typical four-year college degree. Although any one of these aforementioned job titles are worth pursuing and offer a high financial reward, the path is not easy; therefore, do not expect to get rich quickly. A significant time commitment is required. The financial reward only comes after several years of academic study, hard work, long hours, and delayed gratification. King Solomon said, "Wealth from get-rich-quick schemes quickly disappears; wealth from hard work grows over time" (Proverbs 13:11).

It is not our Creator's will for everyone to have the same mental abilities, physical skills, and inclinations. It is not suitable or practical for everyone to become a doctor, lawyer, or investment banker. Does this mean that someone with a more

111

"white-collar" job will always earn more than someone that performs "blue-collar" work? On the contrary. Our Creator saw fit to ensure that a person's ability to obtain wealth, or earn a high wage, is not dependent on the number of years spent in school or the number of degrees obtained. While a surgeon and an auto mechanic may not have much in common outside of repairing something physical, the jobs have one major similarity. In order to continue earning a wage, both must trade their time for money if they want to continue earning an income. The moment that either stops working, they will cease earning a salary.

If you want real wealth, which is derived from a re-occurring sustainable income that will continue to be earned when you cease working, you must escape the black hole of continuously trading time for dollars.

Time Value Of Money

Everything that is finite, having bounds or limits, has a value that can be attached to it. Our world is defined by time and space. There is only so much time and space that is available to us. We all have an expiry date when we will cease to know time and occupy livable space. Before that moment occurs, we are all blessed with a valuable gift called time – and it's up to us to determine how we use it.

Because your time on earth is limited, there is a set number of minutes, hours, days, weeks, months, and years available for you to earn money. Once time is gone, you cannot get it back. No matter how much you would like to get back lost time, it's gone forever. Therefore, lost time is lost money. Waste time and you forfeit available earning potential. As that old saying goes – time is money.

Anyone that has taken a finance or accounting course has probably studied a concept called the time value of money, which is often referred to as TVM. TVM is the idea that money available today, or at the present, has a higher value than the same amount in the future due to its current earning potential. There are several books and financial calculators in circulation to help students learn TVM principles. TVM can also be found in children cartoons. Without knowing it, you were learning TVM watching *Popeye* cartoons whenever you heard Popeye's friend Wimpy say, "I would gladly pay you Tuesday for a hamburger today." Wimpy, who enjoys hamburgers as much as Popeye likes spinach, understood that a full stomach today provides the necessary energy needed for labor to pay tomorrow's obligations. When you thoroughly understand the power of TVM and apply its principals to your daily life by becoming a master over time, or a *Time Lord,* as I like to call it, wealth will soon be at your doorstep.

How do you become a *Time Lord*, making time work for you instead of you being a slave to time?

Advancements in technology have made this possible.

Consider two people working as high school teachers – one is 55 years old and the other is 35. They both teach math at the same school, hold only one university degree, and have been teaching for 13 years. They both spend an additional three hours providing tutoring each day for which they are paid. The elder teacher earns $60,000 a year and the younger $300,000.

How is this possible when they both spend the same amount of time teaching and have no other income outside of teaching?

The younger teacher better understands TVM and has become a *Time Lord,* a master of his time.

How does he do it?

The older teacher provides tutoring during an afterschool enrichment program and is paid for this service. The younger teacher provides after-school tutoring but uses a different forum. Instead of teaching a small group of kids in a classroom, the younger teacher live streams videos and offers prior recordings of tutoring sessions to paid subscribers through his website. The content is also available on DVD for purchase. After eight years of offering this service, the younger teacher has managed to obtain a substantial number of followers and subscribers. His three hours of tutoring each day are multiplied many times over because he has learned how to hold time hostage – capturing time and reserving it for later use. While the elder teacher exchanges his time for dollars, the younger teacher has become a *Time Lord* by finding a way to capture time, which would otherwise be lost, and reuse it to create a reoccurring source of income.

The concept explained above is not new. It has been used by Hollywood to create billions of dollars in revenue and has turned directors, producers, and actors into multi-millionaires. The *smart money* knows that performing stage plays and doing live theater is not where the real money lies. They know that the big money is in the mass distribution of their performances via multiple media outlets such as movies, rentals, cable television, downloads, and the like. The *smart money* structures their contracts in such a way that, not only will they get paid for participating in the movie, they will continue to receive royalties (residual income) long after the movie has stopped showing in theaters. Every time someone purchases the DVD, downloads or watches the movie on pay-for-view, the *smart money* gets paid. Technology makes this possible by capturing all the hours and work spent to create the movie on a storable media device, allowing an end-user to view it later for a small fee.

The music industry operates in the same manner and is rewarded handsomely by making billions in sales each year. However, stage performances and tours in select cities are not where the bulk of a professional singer's money is made. The *smart money* will own the rights to their music and make money each time someone purchases their music. Whereas the number of fans a singer can reach while performing on tour is limited by time, space, and the affordability of the ticket, there are fewer constraints on the number of paid downloads or CDs they can sell if the demand is present. Manufacturers will simply increase production to meet demand. Many singers, even dead ones, are still making money many years after they initially recorded the music. The *smart money* fully understands TVM and have mastered the techniques used by other *Time Lords* to create a residual stream of income to build long-term wealth.

The *Time Lords* discussed above have benefited by applying one extremely important money-making principle – they stopped trading time for dollars. There was the initial outlay of labor and time needed to produce the video, movie, or song, but because of technology, no further effort or time commitment is required of them to earn money. This enables them to direct their time towards other income-producing endeavors. The key principle to learn from this is to do something only once but continue to make money from your labor long after the initial work is completed. This is not lazy; it's just smart.

THREE FORMS OF INCOME

The Internal Revenue Service (IRS) categorizes income into three broad types: active income, passive income, and portfolio income. While all three are suitable for making money, passive income and portfolio income are preferred over active income because of the smaller time commitment required.

Most people are familiar with active income – income received from performing a service. This includes the bulk of work performed and includes wages, tips, salaries, commissions, and income from business in which there is meaningful participation. Active income is great if you want to stay in the rat race of trading time for dollars.

Passive income is defined as *income that is received on a regular basis, with little effort required to maintain it.* This is how the *smart money* makes money. But understand, there is no such thing as 100% passive income; sitting back and doing nothing as you watch the money roll in. There is the initial labor that is required by you, or someone else, that can be quite substantial. Even with real estate, someone has to manage the properties. However, after the process is automated, maintaining things becomes a lot easier. Passive income is working smarter, not harder for money.

Portfolio income is derived from various forms of investments such as stocks, bonds, mutual funds, and annuities. The income from these types of investments includes interest, dividends, and capital gains. Royalties from investment property are also included in portfolio income. Establishing portfolio income for yourself is the next step after successfully creating multiple sources of passive income.

THE BENEFITS OF PASSIVE INCOME

Passive income is not new. It has been around for a very long time. Sticking to our principle of creating income with little or no effort to maintain it, let's explore, in detail, one important man that utilized a semi-passive income strategy to create substantial wealth. We will review the life of Abraham, a man known for his righteousness and great wealth.

Abraham was very rich in livestock, silver, and gold (Genesis 13:2), but the bulk of his wealth consisted of cattle and livestock – a form of passive income that would continue to increase, enhancing his wealth. There was the initial outlay of time and resources to obtain the cattle and livestock, along with a bit of luck; but after it was acquired, very little ongoing effort on Abraham's part was required to manage and grow his investment. All he had to do was wait on the birth of their offspring. Abraham's grandson, Jacob, obtained his wealth in a similar manner when he was working for Laban, his mother's brother. The same technique can work today.

Some people will not consider raising cattle and livestock as passive income. But remember, passive income is a residual income that you continue to receive with little or no effort to maintain it. Abraham's servants were primarily responsible for ensuring that his livestock had access to green pastures, water, and to keep predators away. Outside of that, the majority of their time was spent watching the sheep, oxen, donkeys, and camels eat grass and produce offspring to be bartered, sold, or consumed. The amount of ongoing work required was minuscule. That sounds a lot like passive income to me – your wealth continues to increase whether or not you do any meaningful work.

This concept is deployed by many people today to obtain passive income.

Consider this example.

A woman, who is passionate about dogs, decides to create passive income for herself by becoming a dog breeder. She purchases three pedigree Chow Chows – two females and one male. At an average cost of $6,000 each, the woman must make an initial investment of $18,000 to purchase the dogs from a reputable breeder. The annual expense for keeping the dogs (i.e., food and veterinarian expense) is $2,000. Therefore, the costs of ownership for the first year is $20,000. After the first year, the dogs are ready for breeding. If each female has five puppies for a total of ten, at a selling price of $6,000 this will provide her $60,000 in revenue. After deducting the $20,000 startup costs incurred during the first year of ownership, our happy dog owner can make roughly $40,000, or a return on investment (ROI) of 200%, in her second year of business. As long as she is a dog owner that breeds pedigree dogs, doing something she loves, she will profit from her investment. This is a simplified, yet realistic, example of the power of passive income and what you can do to work smarter, not harder, for more residual income.

CHAPTER SUMMARY

Trading time for dollars is not an efficient way to earn money. Your objective should be to identify a task that only requires one initial outlay of labor, but once you have completed it you can continue to derive a reoccurring source of revenue from it. This is the time value of money principle at work and it has made many people who have mastered this principle wealthy. The principle is simple to enact. Work smarter, not harder, by harnessing the power of technology to capture time and sell your product or service over-and-over again.

There are three forms of income recognized by the Internal Revenue Service: active income, passive income, and portfolio income. Between active income and passive income, passive income is preferred because passive income allows you to be paid even when you are no longer actively working. Passive income may require a lot of upfront work to get the ball rolling, but once you get things established you reach a point where only a minimal amount of effort is needed to maintain this income stream, and the money will continue to flow in. By contrast, active income is money that stops coming in once you stop working. If you quit your job or are laid off, you will stop being paid. Once you have several forms of passive income streams working for you, you can begin investing in developing portfolio income.

9

MIND YOUR OWN BUSINESS

Every boss started as a worker. – Moosa Rahat

It is always a great honor to be the driver of your own car, to be the boss of your own fate! – Mehmet Murat ildan

You'll never make a fortune working for the boss man. – Jeanette Walls

There is a travesty I have observed with seemingly no end; well-qualified men and women with advanced university degrees are unable to find suitable employment commensurate with their qualifications. This is something all too familiar to minority groups and women living in the United States and abroad. Quite often, the obstacle preventing them from finding suitable employment is not their own creation. This is the work of social conditioning and hidden biases working to erode the ladder of opportunity and economic progress.

The aforementioned demographic groups described above did not foresee this happening, for only a fool would spend so much of their time, energy, and resources to pursue a path, that takes years to complete, if it offered little opportunity for monetary reward and financial advancement. They listened to their most trusted advisors – parents, relatives, and mentors – tell stories of being denied promotion and advancement, because they were considered unqualified, because they lacked a certain degree, despite having several years of specific industry or work-related experience. Not wanting to receive a similar outcome, hundreds of thousands of talented young

121

people followed the guidance of good-hearted, well-meaning advisors by pursuing an advanced university degree in order to become more qualified and eligible for senior positions. Instead of receiving a high-paying job and access to a brighter future, what they received is debilitating student loan debt and a new excuse for why they are denied a job or a promotion.

Unknown to them, the "system" adapted to the change that was occurring. No longer able to deny candidates for hire or promotion by using the excuse that they do not have the requisite education, they found a new reason to exclude, one that is more subjective but is unlikely to result in complaints of discrimination. Instead of saying, "We are looking for someone with these specific qualifications," those making the ultimate hiring decision will say that they are looking for "the right fit." These words are a dog whistle to the trained ear. What they truly mean to say is, "We cannot deny that you are qualified; however, there is something about you that makes us feel uncomfortable, but we are unwilling to say it openly because it would make us appear racist or sexist. You are not one of us. We are going to hire someone that we have more in common with, and who will make us feel more comfortable living with our biases and discriminatory opinions."

COLLEGE GRADUATES

There are legions of fresh graduates and experienced candidates that are passed over each year – denied jobs because they were told the company is looking for "the right fit" even though they possess all the desired skills and were deemed qualified, having passed the initial screen of Human Resources or the search firm contracted to find suitable candidates. After spending months, and even years, searching for a job and going to numerous interviews, they find themselves in an undesirable position – unemployed, underemployed, and often deep in debt.

The people that followed the advice given to them by making the decision to advance their education, in an effort to become better qualified, did not make a mistake or a bad decision. A commitment to learning is never wrong. However, it is the assumption and expectation that someone will do for you what you are unwilling to do for yourself that is open to criticism. The assumption is that someone will give you a job instead of you creating one for yourself.

It's extremely important before embarking on a course of study that you determine whether, upon receipt of your degree or certificate, the education received will make you fit to pursue self-employment or obtain contract work, if the need arises. During your matriculation through college or university, you should actively think of ways to procure a living wage for yourself if the opportunity to gain suitable employment is not available. There are still far too many college graduates living in their parent's home because they are unable to find a job that pays a living wage.

EXPERIENCED PROFESSIONALS

Another occurrence that happens frequently is competent men and women give 10-plus years to a company with the hope of climbing the corporate ladder and receiving a coveted title. Unfortunately, many of them will leave the company feeling bitter, angry, and frustrated. It should be noted that a very small percentage of this group will receive a promotion, reaching the level of middle management. However, the majority of them will be unable to advance to more senior positions by breaking the glass ceiling above them, despite the fact that they are well respected and regarded in the company as a valuable and trusted resource. In all but a few cases, they will be passed over by less competent employees who did not work as hard but are liked by a "sponsor" who can advance their career. This situation occurs too many times and is prevalent in companies and job industries all over the world where favoritism is preferred over hard work and measurable accomplishments.

Whenever a person, a collective group of people, or a company, by their repeated actions express who they are, you had better believe them. Do not believe that you will be treated differently. Do not trust that you can change the attitude, thoughts, and the heart of corrupt people by your actions and hard work alone. This is a work for God to perform.

What if ambitious, hard-working employees, instead of spending valuable time laboring for an employer, toiling late into the night and working weekends to affect someone else's bottom line, direct their efforts into minding their own business?

Long-term, I believe the outcome will be far more rewarding.

A short, yet powerful poem written by Suzy Kassem summarizes this point.

THE THREE BEES

A young boy once asked
A wealthy beekeeper:
"What is the secret of
Your success?"
The beekeeper simply smiled
And replied:

"To be successful,
One has to be one of three bees,
The queen bee,
The hardest working bee,
Or the bee that does not fit in.
One success is inherited,
And the next one is earned.
While the last one is
Self-Sought,
Self-Served,
And happens own its own
Terms."

"And which one are you?"
Asked the boy.
The beekeeper then wiped
The sweat from his head
And said:
"The last may seem the riskiest,
But the glory of achievement
Is the most rewarding.
Freedom always comes at a high cost,
But only when you are
Your own boss,
Can you truly
Afford it."

START YOUR OWN BUSINESS

You can get rich working for someone else, but you will not become wealthy unless you have something you own working for you. Many people will not understand this truth because they do not know the difference between being rich as opposed to being wealthy. They believe that being rich and being wealthy are synonymous; however, there is a big difference between the two.

125

Most rich people make a lot of money because of a high salary, but the moment they stop working, they stop making money because the source of their income is gone. A wealthy person does not physically have to work to make money. A rich person has to physically work to earn money whereas a wealthy person has sustainable sources of income that can last for years through asset investments producing reoccurring streams of income. It's this form of prosperity that we should seek. As Henry Ford once said, "The only prosperity the people can afford to be satisfied with is the kind that lasts."

Being wealthy is defined as *the status of an individual's existing financial resources that supports his or her standard of living or way of life for an undefined duration, even if they do not physically labor to generate a recurring income.* Wealth is measured by time and not by how much money one has.

The main difference between being rich and being wealthy is knowledge. Wealthy people know how to make money while rich people only have money. For example, a person can become rich in an instant by winning the lottery or by receiving an inheritance. However, this type of wealth is also easily lost. There are numerous examples of financially illiterate lottery winners and people who received a large inheritance losing it very quickly. Real wealth is obtained over a period of years from assets and by developing sustainable streams of income. While both rich and wealthy people may experience hardships and failures in their pursuits, wealthy people are more knowledgeable when it comes to money matters. A wealthy person knows how to start over again and rebuild the wealth that was lost. In contrast, it will be more difficult for a rich person to do the same. Therefore, one should strive to be wealthy instead of rich. Rich people are motivated by money whereas wealthy people are motivated by their aspirations, purpose, and passions.

To avoid the risk of being disappointed and losing precious years of earning potential by working for someone else, everyone should consider starting their own business to accumulate long-term wealth. As long as someone other than yourself employs you, the amount of money you can make is capped. Your employer will determine your basic salary and bonus. If you have stock options, even the number of your options is determined by someone else. But when you work for yourself, you set your own wage, salary, and bonus. There is no cap on your earning potential. Moreover, when you own your own business you are accumulating wealth. As your business expands by adding more distribution channels, increasing the number of products offered, and growing the customer base, profitability increases along with the value of your business.

A time may come when you decide to sell your business. It's at this point when the value of your business is fully recognized – when the accumulated equity is converted into cash. Most cash millionaires, business owners that have millions in liquid assets, did not accumulate their cash by paying themselves a high salary. The cash is received when the business is sold. This is how the majority of small business owners become millionaires. The process is similar to flipping a house.

Flipping a house is when an investor purchases an undervalued property and makes a profit when it is sold. In many cases, the property is in a dilapidated condition making it unfit to occupy. The investor will renovate the property making key upgrades to the kitchen, bathrooms, and appliances to increase the value of the property. Once the renovations are completed, the property is listed for sale at a price much higher than the original purchase price. When a buyer purchases the property, the investor profits from the sale by receiving the equity that was added by the renovations. The investor may decide to use the cash received from the sale for personal use, but most of the time the proceeds are used to purchase other undervalued properties and the process is repeated.

Make no mistake; operating your own business is not easy. There is a lot of hard work involved. However, being an employee can be equally difficult but without the financial upside. If the company you work for is sold or merges with another company, you get nothing in return and may end up without a job in an effort to eliminate redundancy. Therefore, everyone should pursue ownership in the company they work for in order to have a claim to the equity if the enterprise is successful and is later sold. Your initial investment may be small, but it will grow in size. If you cannot be one of the principal owners because you work for a publicly traded company, you should buy the company's stock. As an aside, if you work for a company and are unwilling to invest in the company's stock, you should seek another employer.

I want to underscore this point. Get ownership in something. Own a piece of whatever you spend the majority of your time doing to make money. This is one of the best ways to accumulate long-term wealth. If time restraints and other important commitments prohibit you from pursuing more active income-producing ventures, you read in previous chapters how investing in passive income strategies can establish the path for wealth accumulation.

DEVELOP YOUR BRAND

While the merits of business ownership have been adequately explained, it's understood that some people are simply better suited to remain employees. There is no shame in working for someone else to earn an honest living. However, if you must work for someone else, while you are in their employment do the best job you can. You will be rewarded, if not in your current job through promotion – bonuses and the like, then in a future endeavor. I am a big believer that hard work and talent will provide a way for itself to stand out. Your hard work and effort will not go unnoticed.

In the world of commerce, there are two kinds of transactions – buying and selling. Sellers compete with other sellers to attract consumers that desire their product or service. Successful sellers are good at marketing their product and service and are good at branding. Branding is the process involved in creating a unique name and image for a product or service in the consumer's mind, mainly through an advertising campaign with a consistent theme. Branding is established each time a customer uses a product or service. The consistency of the product or service received reinforces the brand in the customer's mind. Therefore, in order to establish a good brand, it's imperative that there is consistency in the product or service offered and the customer experience.

McDonald's and Coca-Cola are two companies good at branding. No matter where you are in the world, the taste of a Big Mac or a Coca-Cola will always be the same. Trust me, a great deal of time and money is spent by both these companies to ensure this remains true. They understand that a brand is established by offering a consistent experience every time a customer purchases their product. If someone purchases a Big Mac or Coca-Cola and it does not taste the same, the quality of the brand is not diminished by this experience. The customer believes that this is a one-off or an anomaly; although possible, the chances of this happening again is extremely unlikely.

The lesson to be learned from this is to guard the brand. Guard it by creating a consistent, repeatable experience so that each time a customer purchases the product or service the quality of the brand is reinforced in their mind. If the customer experience is inconsistent, the brand will never be established or it will diminish. Neither outcome is favorable, as they both will lead to lower customer satisfaction, sales, and profitability.

Many people fail to realize, that even though they may not be directly involved in selling a product or service, they are actively involved in selling something every day – that something is themselves. Whatever work you are engaged in, you are developing a brand. Each time someone encounters you or has an opportunity to evaluate you or your work, you are developing your brand. You are creating expectations and shaping the way you are perceived. Therefore, guard your brand. Take pride in your work. Whatever job you have to do, give your level best to make sure that it's done right. Don't settle for good enough; good enough isn't good enough if it can be better and better isn't good enough if it can be best. Protect your brand by dedicating yourself to excellence. Excellence should be a habit, not an act because you are what you repeatedly do. Protect your brand by making sure you arrive to work on time each day. Turn in your deliverables as early as possible and do the job in less time than required without sacrificing quality or content. Make this statement your motto, "I would rather be an hour early than a minute late." Give your boss or employer more in work and added value than what you receive in salary. Always speak in a professional manner. Take note of your appearance ensuring that your clothes are neat and clean and that you are always well groomed.

If you are mindful to develop a quality brand and reputation, trust that you are establishing unforeseen opportunities for advancement. There is a great need for dependable, trustworthy, reliable people who will give their very best each time a task is presented. Those who can are generally well compensated; if not in their current employment, they will when another opportunity arises. When another opportunity appears, your work ethic will have established your readiness and your success is assured – not because of luck or favor, but because of your preparation. Luck is best defined as *when preparation meets opportunity*.

Chapter Summary

You can become rich working for someone else, but it will be very difficult for you to become wealthy. As long as you work for someone other than yourself, you are never completely in charge of your salary or the tenure of your employment. The amount of money you make is capped by your employer, and there is no guarantee that you will be promoted to a more senior position. This is not the path to real wealth. Wealthy people do not rely on salaried income to maintain their standard of living.

Many college graduates and experienced professionals are often disappointed when they expect an employer to offer them a job or reward them for several years of labor. Working for a company appears less risky than starting your own business, but ask anyone that has ever been laid off and they will tell you that there is no such thing as a guaranteed job or paycheck. Both have a degree of risk, but the benefits of one far outweigh the other and have unlimited upside.

If you must work for someone other than yourself, be the best at what you do. Establish a reputation for doing good work. Be your own brand; therefore, establish a brand you can be proud of. A quality reputation and brand are the best forms of marketing you can do for yourself.

10

MULTIPLE STREAMS OF INCOME

Lack of money is the root of all evil. – George Bernard Shaw

Plant your seed in the morning and keep busy all afternoon, for you don't know if profit will come from one activity or another – or maybe both. – King Solomon

Income, that is the thing. I wish an income that will keep flowing into my purse whether I sit on the wall or travel to far lands. – George S. Clason, The Richest Man In Babylon

In the preceding chapter, you learned the benefits of owning your own business versus working for someone else. This chapter will discuss the importance of having more than one stream of income.

ECONOMIC UNCERTAINTY

There will always be periods of economic uncertainty. All throughout recorded history, the business cycle has created periods of economic booms and busts. Money is made and money is lost – rather, money is transferred to someone else. There are periods of inflation and periods of deflation. The volatility of the market affects everyone. The magnitude at which it affects your quality of life is largely dependent upon how much money you have saved and the quality and velocity of your cash flow – how quickly your money is acquired and exchanged. If you are not privately wealthy, in order to protect yourself against times of economic uncertainty, it's imperative that you have multiple sources of income to draw from. Every working adult and family should have an extra income that serves as an insurance policy against hard times.

It should be made clear that a second income is not an emergency fund. An emergency fund is an account made up of cash or highly liquid assets that are available for use during an unexpected personal financial setback, such as job loss, a debilitating illness, or a major expense. The amount of cash needed in an emergency fund is a personal decision, but financial advisors typically suggest sufficient cash to cover at least three months of living expenses. Having an emergency fund is sound advice, but this is not enough. You also need an extra source of income.

Matter is constantly in motion. Nothing remains in a static state. The same is true for money – it is either increasing or decreasing in value. Money held in low-yielding savings accounts or locked in a safe will lose value over time due to inflation. Because the value of the asset(s) held in an emergency fund can decline, it cannot be fully trusted. In order to protect your financial well-being something more is needed.

Job Loss

Imagine a 48-year old man married with two children ages 16 and 14. The man is a senior executive and has enjoyed an 18-year career working for a large regional bank. He is paid a $150,000 annual salary and receives a 20% bonus bringing his total compensation to $180,000. The bank, and the department he manages, has performed well in past years and his boss promised him a promotion at year-end. The promotion will bring his salary to $200,000. His wife has not worked since the kids were born and she spends most of her free time volunteering at their school and the church the family attends. The oldest child is a sophomore in high school and is preparing to attend the same private liberal arts college in Massachusetts his parents attended.

Fast forward one year. With his recent promotion, the man has upgraded the family's socioeconomic status by moving into a nicer, more expensive home in a gated community. After driving a minivan for the last eight years, to take the kids and their friends to after-school activities, the wife has decided to trade in the van for a luxury sedan and our banker has decided to buy himself a similar vehicle. Life could not be better for them. However, things are not so good at the bank. The economy is in recession and it has become increasingly difficult for banks to report a profit. The financial pundits and talking heads on television have suggested that banks may need to merge in order to create synergies that will drive down costs and create a path for higher profitability.

Fast forward one more year. The man is now 50 and his eldest child is preparing to start college in the fall. The bank announced plans to merge with another regional bank and will restructure the organization by cutting 2,000 jobs to eliminate redundancies. Unfortunately, the senior manager discussed above is included in these job cuts.

And just like that, the reality for this family has suddenly changed – taking a turn for the worse. The primary breadwinner has lost his job eliminating the family's only income. Favorably, the family has an emergency fund to cover three months of living expenses, but with the job market in such a bad state and other banks cutting back on staff, the prospects of finding another job paying a similar salary are very uncertain. Very soon, the family will have to make some very important decisions and adjust their lifestyle and spending.

What will this look like and what effect will it have on this family?

This is the family's new reality.

Everyone is under a great deal of stress. Our former banker is concerned about the length of time it will take to find another job. He has reached out to all of his contacts, but no companies are hiring. His wife is worried about how long the emergency fund will last to pay bills; now they have two car payments coupled with a higher mortgage. Additionally, because of the high income the family reported on their eldest child's college application, they qualify for only a small amount of financial aid.

They will need to do a material restructuring in order to cut expenses and lengthen the sustainability of their emergency fund. Gone are the family nights eating out at their favorite restaurant, the daily trip to Starbucks in the morning, weekend trips to the mall; these are the easiest changes to make. The hardest decision affects their oldest child. No longer able to afford the private school in Boston, they will have to attend a local community college or defer enrollment at his parent's alma mater for one year – all because someone at the bank with a more senior position made a decision to eliminate their father's job.

Although this is a hypothetical story, this scenario has happened before bringing grief to single individuals and families alike. Losing a job can cause significant emotional hardship, causing depression, worry, stress, tearing apart marriages, adversely affecting adults and innocent children. While job loss can happen to anyone, minorities suffer disproportionately more than whites because they generally have less money saved to cushion the blow.

Some of you will probably take issue with this story, arguing that the family described in this example represents a very small percentage of families. I acknowledge there used to be a time when more families could live fairly well on one income. The man of the house would go to work and the woman would remain home to look after the kids and perform the difficult task of maintaining the home. If the wife wanted a little extra money to pay for small purchases or to put away for savings, she would work a part-time job, but this was not generally necessary because her husband made enough money from his job to furnish their needs. Unfortunately, this lifestyle is no longer that common and has been replaced with each adult member of the household needing to work a full-time job in order to make ends meet, let alone put away money for savings. The sad reality is that it now takes two wage earners to support a family, whereas a generation ago it only required one. For many families, the struggle to earn a living is real.

DUAL INCOMES

Heed these words! Never allow yourself to be put in the above situation, where someone can possess this much influence over your financial future and mental health, because you only have one source of income. Therefore, it's imperative that you have another source of income to fall back on as this will provide much-needed cash flow and reduce the drain on savings, particularly if you, or the primary wage earner, lose a job. Although the second income may not be sufficient to meet all your financial needs if a job loss does occur, psychologically, it will at least provide some level of mental support, because you will not have to worry as much about how you will pay for necessities - such as food and utilities.

I saw this principle carried out when I lived near Washington, DC. I frequently met middle-aged adults, some single and others married, that had a side hustle for extra income. Many were very well educated and earned a good income from their full-time job, but because of economic uncertainty and the high cost of living in an expensive city, many pursued a secondary source of income in order to live more comfortably – to eat out at restaurants, have money to travel, and to fund retirement accounts.

It was common for people to ask, "What do you do and where do you work."

After responding, I typically asked the same. If the conversation went well, I usually asked them for their business card, expecting to see their job title and the name of their employer. Instead, most of the time they gave me a business card referencing their side hustle.

Initially, I falsely believed that most of the people I encountered were simply greedy. In Omaha, Nebraska, where I am from, well-educated people with good jobs did not have a side hustle. I later learned that people living in expensive cities firmly understand the importance of secondary cash flow, and will work to obtain it, even if it seems unneeded.

Allow me to directly address couples.

If one of you is fortunate to not have to work because your significant other makes enough income to meet your household's needs, I still encourage you to have another source of income because two incomes are generally better than one, and often helps to strengthen the union.

This truth is made clear in a series of verses found in Proverbs 31:10-31, known to many readers as the virtuous woman because it describes a certain woman and her many virtues. One of her virtues, apart from being skillful at managing her time, and that of others, is that her hands are never idle. Not required or needing to work, she is a blessing to her husband and is a contributor to the family wealth. She is a woman with a keen financial mind and is able to make sound financial investments. She is knowledgeable and able to spot good deals and purchase assets at a reasonable price to ensure that her business activities are always profitable. She uses the proceeds she earns from her investments to pursue other sustainable assets that will produce an ongoing source of income for the years to come.

There are powerful life lessons and lessons about time management, thrift, investing, and creating generational wealth within these 21 verses. Worth noting, the virtuous woman had a well-developed strategy to use passive income as a means to obtain wealth.

Women and men, young adults and senior citizens, can equally benefit from developing a passive income strategy. For retirees on a fixed income, the presence of multiple sources of passive income will help to relieve any stress and anxiety caused by wondering whether retirement income will be sufficient to maintain financial independence and a respectable quality of life. For retirees with investment accounts, passive income streams will help prolong the duration of retirement accounts such as 401(k) plans, a 403(b), and individual retirement accounts (IRAs). Passive income is an untapped diamond mine stocked with wealth creating opportunities that lie waiting for you to discover.

The point I want to make clear is that multiple income sources are generally better than one. Obtaining another source of income may mean that you have to become more creative with your time by working smarter, not harder. There are only 24 hours in a day and some of that time is needed for eating, sleeping, spending time with family, or maintaining a social life. There must be a balance. Chapter 8 discussed a solution to this common problem – not enough time in the day and maintaining balance.

BUILDING BIGGER BARNS

Some will rightly question, if you do not need the money, what is the point of committing precious time to create multiple streams of income?

Isn't this being greedy?

Instead of building "bigger barns" isn't your time better spent investing in people and relationships? Aren't these things more important than money?

This is a reasonable conclusion. However, there is a time for everything and there is a time when it is necessary to defer developing certain kinds of relationships. This will be explained in a later chapter. For now, let me explain what is meant by "bigger barns" by explaining the Parable of the Rich Fool found in Luke 12.

In verse 15, Jesus tells the multitude, "Beware! Guard against every kind of greed. Life is not measured by how much you own." Then he tells them a short story.

"A rich man had a fertile farm that produced fine crops. He said to himself, 'What should I do? I don't have room for all my crops.' Then he said, 'I know! I'll tear down my barns and build bigger ones. Then I'll have room enough to store all my wheat and other goods. And I'll sit back and say to myself, "My friend, you have enough stored away for years to come. Now take it easy! Eat, drink, and be merry!" "But God said to him, 'You fool! You will die this very night. Then who will get everything you worked for?' "Yes, a person is a fool to store up earthly wealth but not have a rich relationship with God" (Luke 12:16-21).

Jesus does not criticize the rich man in the parable for being wealthy. The fact that he has abundance and has prospered is not the reason for his criticism. The condemnation comes from not using his abundance to benefit others. There is no mention of family or friends that he intends to share his wealth with. He plans to use and enjoy his additional riches privately, exclusive of others! This is what is meant by not having a rich relationship with God.

Helping others is the duty of man and is a moral responsibility.

Paul, in his second letter to the Corinthians, said,

"Right now you have plenty and can help those who are in need. Later, they will have plenty and can share with you when you need it. In this way, things will be equal" (2 Corinthians 8:14). "For God is the one who provides seed for the farmer and then bread to eat. In the same way, he will provide and increase your resources and then produce a great harvest of generosity in you. Yes, you will be enriched in every way so that you can always be generous. And when we take your gifts to those who need them, they will thank God" (2 Corinthians 9:10-12).

All too often we error by assuming that God has increased our income to raise our standard of living when the reason for our blessing is for us to increase our standard of giving. Because human beings are extremely diverse with unequal talents and abilities, some people do not possess the physical ability or mindset that is needed to make a lot of money. They are gifted in other areas that add to the beauty of this world, and we are enriched by their service. Others are gifted with the intellectual capacity and physical ability to make enormous sums of money. The problem occurs when their desire for personal gratification greatly exceeds their generosity and their wealth is not shared with the less fortunate.

There is nothing inherently wrong with money or pursuing additional income opportunities, nor is there anything wrong with possessing the knowledge and ability to create multiple streams of income. These attributes do not make you greedy. Indeed, they should be viewed as gifts from God; therefore, you are expected to use these gifts to the best of your ability. However, if your "barn" has reached its capacity and is about to burst because your income now exceeds your needs and reasonable wants, then it's time for you to start thinking of ways to benefit others with your abundance instead of indulging yourself.

Charity starts at home. Start by ensuring that your immediate family and close relatives are provided for. Then look out for your friends and neighbors. Donate the excess money you earn to an orphanage, homeless shelter, food pantry, schools, museums, national parks and recreations, etc. Create a scholarship fund for worthy students. There are numerous ways the money can be utilized to bless others. If, for some reason, you consider philanthropy a handout, then provide an aspiring entrepreneur with an interest-free loan to help them become their own boss. Be very careful of building "bigger barns" for yourself when there are people that you can help.

A Rising Tide

There is an expression that says a rising tide lifts all boats. I observed this saying to be quite true during my stay in the Middle East.

The United Arab Emirates (UAE) is a small oil-rich country located in the Middle East. At the time of this writing, it was the eighth largest Middle Eastern country with a population estimate of 9.54 million. Of this amount, approximately 88% of the country's residents are expatriates living and working on an employment visa. Despite a relatively small population, the UAE has accomplished a great deal since forming in 1971. Dubai, the largest city by population, is recognized as a top travel destination around the world, has a diversified economy, and can boast of having the tallest building in the world. A large number of skilled professionals and laborers are needed to sustain the country's robust growth. Therefore, people from all over the world, including advanced countries like the United States of America, United Kingdom, Canada, Australia, and New Zealand, and developing countries such as India, Pakistan, Bangladesh, and the Philippines, come to the UAE, and to the other oil-rich countries that make up the Gulf Cooperation Council (GCC), to work.

There are times when it seems that some of the jobs people have are superfluous. Most companies, no matter their size, have an office boy, tea boy, and a driver. Go to any mall or hypermarket and it always appears overstaffed with excessive employees standing around waiting for a customer to assist. The city streets are kept clean and the vegetation and shrubbery aligning the highways and streets are kept in a well-manicured state due to hundreds of street cleaners. The average Emirati family often has several nannies and housemaids to assist with raising children and maintaining the home. This abundant lifestyle was made possible because of the wisdom and benevolence of a great leader, the late Father of the Nation Sheikh Zayed bin Khalifah Al Nahyan, and the wealth that comes from having a vast supply of oil.

I found myself asking, "Why did God bless some countries in the Middle East with so much wealth enabling its citizens to enjoy such a high standard of living?"

Before answering, I must mention that there are several countries in Africa that have an abundance of oil, gold, diamonds, and other precious minerals. For example, Sierra Leone is one of the world's poorest countries despite being one of the largest diamond exporters. It also has a vast amount of minerals. Due to greed, corruption, theft, and fiscal mismanagement, only the country's leaders and a few families live extremely well while the rest of the country lives in poverty. The major difference between some Middle Eastern and African countries is that the leaders did not hoard the wealth to themselves but shared it with its citizens.

After much reflection and observation, I came to the realization that the wealth in the Middle East is a part of God's divine plan to provide for basic human needs. These Arab countries provide a great benefit to the world by offering the many foreigners that live within its borders something they would lack in their home country – employment, and the chance to earn a higher wage. The salary these expats earn is often enough to allow them to build a house back home and provide for several family members, pay the costs of tuition, and pay off debts. For example, the salary paid to an office boy from India, a housemaid from Ethiopia, a nanny from the Philippines, and a taxi driver from Pakistan, is a large amount compared to what they would earn back home. Without a job in the Middle East, these individuals would have a much different life – the many men and women that come to work would not be able to provide for their children and aging parents.

The wealth in the Middle East is a blessing to the region, creating a rising tide that lifts all boats by raising the standard of living of nationals from other countries. Because the country's leaders shared the nation's wealth with its citizens first, instead of keeping it all for themselves, they were able to create a booming economy where each person could benefit and provide employment to people from surrounding countries. This is the outcome when wealth is shared. An open hand helps more people than a closed fist. It's proof that God uses, and needs, people that know how to use and manage wealth; thereby, creating multiple streams of income, for His glory.

CHAPTER SUMMARY

Multiple streams of income are vital for financial preservation and serve as a shield against economic uncertainty caused by unplanned and unforeseeable events. Just like an emergency fund, multiple streams of income help to sustain you through times of financial stress caused by job loss, illness, and even divorce. The benefits extend beyond periods of financial hardship. Multiple streams of income can supplement social security income, pensions, and prolong the duration of financial retirement accounts.

There is nothing immoral or shameful about committing time to create multiple sources of income, and there is no shame or condemnation for having multiple streams of income and living an abundant lifestyle. If you have the aptitude, the know-how, and the ability to expand your income creating channels, then you should avail yourself of the opportunities that are presented. Use your God-given talents to the best of your ability. This includes the ability to make large sums of money.

Be thankful for any success you may achieve and take time to enjoy the fruits of your labor. However, when the income from your enterprises exceeds any reasonable level of human consumption, remember to be mindful and considerate of those that are less fortunate and who lack basic necessities. You have a moral obligation to meet the needs of others with the excess of your abundance. Don't allow selfishness to corrupt your spirit by hoarding precious resources that, if applied generously, could help others. Acknowledge and understand the difference between Sierra Leone and the United Arab Emirates. Both were blessed with considerable natural resources buried beneath the earth. One exports diamonds and the other oil. However, one country is poor and the other is rich because its leaders had vastly different mindsets and contrasting levels of generosity. One had a spirit of greed and stagnation that manifest itself in high unemployment, the other a spirit of benevolence and growth that created employment opportunities for people from all over the world.

PART 3

THE IMPORTANCE OF RELATIONSHIPS

When we put God first, all other things fall into their proper place or drop out of our lives. Our love of the Lord will govern the claims for our affection, the demands on our time, the interest we pursue, and the order of our priorities. – Ezra Taft Benson

Real relationships are the product of time spent, which is why so many of us have so few of them. – Craig D. Lounsbrough

Things which matter most must never be at the mercy of things that matter least. – Johann Wolfgang von Goethe

11

DEFER SOME RELATIONSHIPS

Marriage can wait, education cannot. – Khaled Hosseini, *A Thousand Splendid Suns*

When God knows you're ready for commitment, He'll reveal the right person under the right circumstances. – Joshua Harris

Our hearts clearly see our own interest but they are completely blind to other people's interest. – Bangambiki Habyarimana

There are times in life when you must place your needs ahead of others. At first glance, this may appear selfish; but in reality, there are occasions when looking after your own interest first is an act of love. There are moments when you are better positioned to provide for the needs of others after you have secured your own. This principle is taught each time you travel on a commercial flight. Before the flight departs, the flight attendant will give a demonstration of how to put on an oxygen mask in the unlikely event of sudden loss of cabin pressure. You are instructed to put your mask on first before you assist others in putting on theirs – including your children. The logic is simple. You are in a better position to assist others after your safety is secured; otherwise, you could all perish.

Many people mistakenly believe that you are morally obligated to put the interest of others ahead of your own. This is not true in all cases. Jesus said in Mark 12:31, "you are to love your neighbor as yourself" and in Luke 6:31 "do to others as you would like them to do to you." Notice these texts do not say love your neighbor more than you love yourself. This would be equivalent to making them a god. Jesus says in John 15:12-13,

> "This is my commandment: Love each other in the same way that I loved you. There is no greater love than to lay down one's life for one's friends."

In case you don't understand what the text attempts to explain, let me provide a bit more context to make it clearer.

Jesus commands us to love in the manner that he has shown love to us. This means never missing an opportunity to help someone if you have the ability to help them. Nowhere in the text does it say that we should die for our neighbors. He clarifies by saying there is *no greater way* to express love than to lay down your life for someone else. Our fellow citizens who risk their lives each day to keep us safe (i.e., military personnel, police officers, and firefighters) personify this kind of love. This is why they are called heroes; they go above and beyond what is generally required.

The love Jesus speaks of must be rightly placed. The Bible instructs you to provide for those in need, but not in all cases – especially if it comes at your family's expense. 1 Timothy 5:8 says, "But those who can't provide for their relatives, especially those of their own household, have denied the faith. Such people are worse than unbelievers." The needs of your family come before the needs of others. It would be irresponsible, and plain stupid, to pay your neighbors rent with money that is needed to pay your own; his family continues to enjoy shelter and your family is put on the street.

It seems the extent to which love is measured, and the manner in which you show love, is highly subjective. If love is expressed best by actions and not words, then there are legitimate times and periods in a person's life when your love must, and should, be self-centered in order to produce the most favorable outcome. This truth is most evident when it comes to pursuing a romantic relationship. You cannot lose sight of your own interests.

MY EXPERIENCE IN COLLEGE

The time spent in college and university is a critical period in a person's life when they should be selfish with their time. During this period, it's best for your time to be undivided.

A reoccurring problem appears on college campuses each year. There are young men and women, full of talent and potential, who are more interested in their hormones than their studies.

For a brief period in college, I was also undisciplined and lacked focus. The efficacy of my study schedule was often determined by the presence of women. If I was studying in my dorm room and a group of young ladies came over, I would put away my books to entertain my attractive guests. If I were studying and my girlfriend called (after she completed her work and was done studying) asking me to visit, I would leave my books because her company was far more interesting and fun. Did my grades suffer because of this? Of course. However, I still managed to pass all my classes. Unfortunately, some of my classmates who did the same did not fare as well. Many of them had to retake classes, which pushed back their graduation date. Meanwhile, the more disciplined young men that were able to focus on their studies, instead of succumbing to their hormones, were able to graduate on time. Not surprisingly, shortly after the graduation ceremony, while they were still wearing their cap and gown, these so-called "nerds" had several attractive women from the neighboring colleges, which they had met during their college matriculation, offer their phone numbers and encourage them to stay in touch.

What I learned from watching this happen over-and-over again is that the men that focused on their studies, instead of pursuing relationships during college, where better off for doing so. When they received their hard-earned degree, they obtained a twofold reward – they got the job offer and the girl, whereas the undisciplined students had to wait another semester or an additional year to graduate, were left watching.

With the added confidence that comes with having a college degree and a well-paying job, these young men were well positioned to reap the benefits of their delayed gratification. By making themselves the priority and selfishly managing their time, they now had the time and resources to focus on obtaining the attention of women that were seemingly out of their league just a few months earlier.

WAIT UNTIL THE TIME IS RIGHT

Derek Sanderson Jeter is a retired future Hall of Fame shortstop that played 20 professional seasons of Major League Baseball (MLB) for the New York Yankees. His professional career ended in 2014. Over the course of his career, Jeter won several personal and team awards. He was chosen to 14 All-Star teams, was awarded the Silver Slugger Award five times, won five Gold Glove awards, two Hank Aaron Awards, was named American League Rookie of the Year, and was a World Champion five times earning the World Series MVP. He won the respect of his teammates, opposing players, and fans. In New York, he was simply referred to as the Captain – holding the title from 2003 until he retired. Jeter's career exemplified class, unlike his troubled teammate Alex Rodriguez whose reputation was marred with controversy over steroid use and extramarital affairs.

The handsome bachelor, and captain of the world champion New York Yankees, was often seen with, and known to have dated, beautiful women. However, Jeter did not get married until 2016 – two years after his playing career ended.

Unlike other male professional athletes, Jeter waited until his playing days were over before he got married. Although these athletes probably have good intentions when they decide to get married during their playing career, the attention they receive from beautiful women is often more than they can handle and they succumb to temptation and commit adultery. While I make no excuse for their infidelity, the temptation is understood. The playing season is very long and is mentally and physically demanding. Half of the season is spent on the road playing in grueling away games. This can cause a tremendous strain on relationships. Communication suffers and the couple grows apart. Cheating is often the underlying reason why the marriage ends in divorce. This is the experience of numerous professional athletes.

It's generally expected for millionaire ballplayers to fully enjoy their years of bachelorhood. Bachelors are seldom condemned for sowing their wild oats. However, once they commit to marriage, they are expected to act like married men and be faithful to their wives. Their responsibilities at home are magnified once children are introduced. It is far better for the athlete to remain single until they are fully ready to commit to marriage and raising children.

The same is true for every man contemplating marriage. If there is another commitment such as work or school, or any competing priority that requires an excessive amount of your time, it may be better to delay getting married. No matter how much money you make, it's not a substitute for time. Your wife and children require your presence and should enjoy spending time with you. If they no longer desire your presence and only look forward to the money you provide, it means you have not been fulfilling your obligation correctly. For a man, it's better to concentrate on your education and career until such time that you are satisfied with your professional status and when your job is less demanding. Favorably, men have time on their side. Men do not have a biological clock that determines when it is best to start a family. A man may be physically able to have children at a young age, but the amount of time needed before he becomes mentally mature and is ready to assume all the responsibilities that come with being a husband and a father take much longer to develop.

Five critical things must be in place before a man is ready for marriage. He must be in a place where he is able to hear and receive God's voice, he must be willing to follow God's instructions, he must have a job, he must acknowledge and accept his role as a cultivator, and finally, he must be a protector. Unless these things are present and firmly established, the chances of maintaining a long-term relationship, without a significant amount of problems, decreases exponentially. Favorably, the second chapter of Genesis provides the blueprint for what every man that is serious about finding a long-term partner should be doing and what every woman who desires a good husband should know.

PRESENCE OF GOD

After God formed Adam and breathed into his nostrils the breath of life, he put the man in a garden eastward in Eden

(Genesis 2:15). The exact location is unknown and actively debated by scholars. There is also dispute over the etymology and meaning of the name Eden. In Hebrew, the noun (Eden) means delight, finery, or luxury. However, there is little debate about what Eden was; it was the garden home in which our first parents dwelt. Therefore, the place where God put Adam was the garden of delight.

God placed Adam in a space where he was best fit – in his presence. Before Adam knew or became familiar with anything else, the first thing he felt was his Creator's presence. This is very important.

A woman should meet a man when he is in the presence of God, a place where he can hear God speak to him. A shared problem that many women have is that they meet a man when he is outside of God's presence, and they try to drag him to a place where he can be around other God-fearing men, like a church, synagogue, or mosque, hoping he will become more refined. This strategy seldom works and is often the beginning of many sorrows and future disappointment.

THE WORD OF GOD

God gave Adam his word – a divine message, telling him not to eat from a particular tree.

> "You may freely eat the fruit of every tree in the garden except the tree of the knowledge of good and evil. If you eat its fruit, you are sure to die" (Genesis 2:16-17).

Notice that a divine message from God and the action of eating occurs in the same sentence. This is significant. Jesus told the devil in Matthew 4:4, "Man shall not live by bread alone, but by every word that proceeds from the mouth of God." Both God's word, a divine message of important instructions, and food are needed to sustain life. Deny yourself either of the two for a prolonged period and you will eventually perish. The word of God sustains your soul's connection to the life giver and food sustains your body.

There are two important lessons in Genesis 2. First, in order for a man to receive God's word, he must recognize the sovereignty of God and be willing to submit to His authority. Secondly, a man must actually follow God's instructions. James 1:22 says, "But be ye doers of the word, and not hearers only, deceiving your own selves." You must actually follow God's word (instructions) to prosper. The key is obedience; a man must have a relationship with God – he must know God personally, and this comes from deliberate and consistent meditation upon God's spoken and written word. He must trust where God leads him and accept the instructions he is given.

A life without the word of God results in death. Adam would later understand what God meant when He said, "Thou shall surely die." The Word of God is life. The Apostle John understood this truth so much it was the opening line in two of the books that he wrote. In John 1:1-4 he says,

> "In the beginning was the Word, and the Word was with God, and the Word was God. The same was in the beginning with God. All things were made by him, and without him was not anything made. In him was life; and the life was the light of men."

In 1 John 1:1 he says,

> "That which was from the beginning, which we have heard, which we have seen with our eyes, which we have looked upon, and our hands have handled, concerning the Word of life."

The command not to eat from the forbidden tree was given to the man, Adam. Adam had the responsibility of making sure he and his wife obeyed God's command. You may recall that when Eve ate the forbidden fruit there was no noticeable change. It was not until her husband, Adam, ate from the forbidden tree that they realized they were naked.

A God-fearing woman desires spiritual leadership from her spouse. She wants him to do to her what God did to Adam; breathe spiritual life into her. Unless a man has God's word and is willing to submit and follow God's instructions, he will fall short of providing the spiritual leadership a woman desires, and his home life will suffer. It is usually when a man stops trusting and looking to God for leadership and direction that things start to go wrong. When problems arise, and they certainly will, how he handles it is when his true character is revealed. Until a man demonstrates that he has a moral compass, guided by a higher power, he is unfit to lead.

WORKING

Before Adam and Eve were introduced, God gave Adam a job. God placed Adam in the garden to work in it and to take care of it. Perhaps Adam did not know it at the time, but the work he performed was preparation for a companion. Because Adam was alone, he had time to focus strictly on securing his environment and building a home without distraction.

Simply put, unless a man has a job he is not ready to be a provider. The amount of money a man makes at a given moment is not as important as the fact that he does indeed have a job. If he is responsible, ambitious, industrious, his wage will eventually increase.

Men were made to work. As I stated in a previous chapter, work is a gift from God. Work functions as a tool to build character – by the sweat from his brow a man learns responsibility, commitment, how to solve problems, and how to work with others. These invaluable traits should be well developed prior to marriage, because marriage will certainly test whether he possess these virtues, and this is not the time to learn on the job.

A man should be settled in his career and financially secure prior to marriage. Anything that will require a significant time commitment should be completed in advance. This way, he has more flexibility to spend time with his spouse who looks forward to spending time with him. There is no rush for a man to get married, and there is no punishment if he waits. Quite the contrary, there are actually benefits for a man to delay marriage.

Women represent a larger percentage of the workforce and there are many women that make more money than men. This is accepted. However, it is still very unnatural, and goes against God's original design, for a woman to leave out for work every day – to put up with work-related stress, unreasonable deadlines, long commutes, office politics, and gender inequality while her "man" is unemployed. Over time, even the most liberal woman will have a problem with this arrangement and will eventually lose respect for him, which will cause problems in their relationship.

Overall, women find a financially secure man more desirable; therefore, a man with this quality has more options and is able to expand the range in the women he elects to pursue. For example, an average looking 35-year old man with a pleasant personality, in reasonably good shape, owns his home, has no debt, and draws an annual salary twice the

160

national average will have little trouble finding a partner. It will be just as easy for him to date a woman that is 15 years younger as it would a woman that is 15 years older. The same would be true if the man's age was 40 or 50. Unfortunately, the same cannot be said for most women. A woman that delays pursuing a marital relationship until her thirties or forties may later regret this decision, particularly if marriage is more important to her than a career. An established career and financial independence is a commendable accomplishment, but numerous studies have shown that these qualities are not what men are most attracted to in women.

CARETAKER AND CULTIVATOR

Adam was the caretaker for the Garden of Eden. He was charged with its maintenance and upkeep. The garden was beautiful and lovely in appearance, but it needed his attention, time, and care to maintain the good work that was started. As the garden's caretaker, Adam probably had a host of duties to perform – chores like pruning plants, transplanting flowers, and training shrubs and bushes to grow in the desired manner. These tasks were demanding but would become more difficult later on.

After Adam and his wife disobeyed God's command not to eat from the forbidden tree, the couple was removed from their garden home and the ground was cursed. No longer would the ground yield desirable plants and vegetation as easily. Adam would have to add cultivator to his list of duties. Now, in addition to pruning and training plants how to grow in a certain way, he has to prepare the soil in order for food to grow. He also has the daunting and repetitive task of picking weeds; undesirable plants that grow in places where they are not wanted and whose presence strains the growth of the more desirable plants. Maintaining a garden is not easy; it's very demanding and physically challenging. It's hard work.

Today, men are still cultivators but in a much different manner.

Think of your life and your environment as a figurative garden. As you grow and mature, many things happen around you that impact and shape your existence. If you choose, you can take a passive approach to life, but just like gardening, to achieve the best results, a more active approach is necessary. Your life, like a garden, needs an active, committed caretaker. It requires you to continuously pick out the weeds by removing the undesirable situations that spring up, which slowly begin to overtake your more pleasurable experiences.

As the future head of a family, a man must recognize and accept his role as caretaker and cultivator of not only his life but also the lives of his wife and children.

As a cultivator, you have to ensure that your wife (like soil) is properly nourished and her life (grow bed) is free from weeds. You have to cover her sometimes to make sure the pressures of life don't make her become hard and dry. You have to give your wife a healthy dose of fertilizer called kindness, love, and attention. If you do this correctly, then the seeds you plant in her will spring forth to become budding plants (children). Your work does not end after planting seeds. As a caretaker, you have to look after your young children making sure they are watered daily with affection and that their tender lives are not damaged by psychologically harming bugs, such as anger, anxiety, depression, dysfunction, fear of failure, and low self-esteem. You have to make sure they form goals (vines) that allow them to stretch beyond their current status and that you support their goals (branches) with your actions and words of encouragement. If you do this, then your children will grow to maturity and produce an abundance of good works in due season.

Keep in mind that God gave Adam, and his offspring, dominion over the earth and everything on it. He gave man the responsibility, and excellent raw materials, to form and create whatever his mind desires. Nowhere in the Bible does it say what God created is "perfect" it says, "It was good"; it was fit for the purpose that it was created. Adam was placed in the Garden of Eden (pleasure). It was not called the Garden of Perfection. It was up to Adam to take the raw material he was given and turn the garden into what his heart desired.

Let me specifically address men.

Your desires are subjective. Therefore, the woman you really want does not yet exist. She is in your mind. Therefore, it's your responsibility to take the beautiful woman you married and lovingly cultivate her into the woman you desire. A woman comes into your life beautiful but incapable of meeting all of your expectations. She needs a bit more development to become the woman of your dreams. She needs you to gently cultivate her, and this may not be easy. Understand that marriage to her will be an arduous, yet highly rewarding, labor of love. Paul admonishes men in Ephesians 5:25-29 to love their wives,

> "Husbands, love your wives, even as Christ also loved the church and gave Himself for her; that He might sanctify and cleanse her with the washing of water by the word, that He might present her to Himself a glorious church, not having spot, or wrinkle, or any such thing; but that she should be holy and without blemish. So husbands ought to love their own wives as their own bodies; he who loves his wife loves

himself. For no man ever hated his own flesh; but nourishes and cherishes it, just as the Lord does the church."

This doesn't mean that you iron out your wife's wrinkles and blemishes in an impatient and hurried manner by yelling at her or by making ultimatums. God forbid. You are to sanctify and cleanse her using the word of God, not by using force. To love your wife means you have to love as God loves; His love is patient and never fails. This means continuously giving of yourself by being consistent in the manner that you love even when their actions suggest that they do not deserve it. The way we are to love is explained in 1 Corinthians 13:4-7. It says,

> "Love is patient, love is kind. It does not envy, it does not boast, it is not proud. It does not dishonor others, it is not self-seeking, it is not easily angered, it keeps no record of wrongs. Love does not delight in evil but rejoices with the truth. It always protects, always trusts, always hopes, always perseveres."

As a caretaker and cultivator, a man is responsible for the welfare and well-being of his wife and children. His effort and leadership will dramatically influence his home life and what his private Garden of Eden will eventually become. A man should thoroughly understand and accept his role as a caretaker and cultivator before getting married or having children.

PROTECTOR

A man should protect his wife and be willing to die for her, if needed. Remember, in marriage, the two have become one flesh. Adam understood this. When God presented Eve to Adam for the very first time, Adam said, "This is now bone of my bones and flesh of my flesh."

164

Jesus offered his life to save the life of his bride – his church. Ephesians 5:30 explains why. It says, "For we are members of his body, of his flesh, and of his bones." We should be willing to follow his example – "After all, no one ever hated their own body, but they feed and care for their body, just as Christ does the church."

CHAPTER SUMMARY

There is an appointed time for everything. The time and conditions when a man chooses to pursue a meaningful relationship with a woman are vitally important. There must be certain things in place in order for the relationship to prosper.

The union of Adam and Eve is a model for you to follow. Until a man is willing and able to demonstrate that he is able to provide five critical things: 1) he is in God's presence; 2) he acknowledges and follows the word of God; 3) he has a job; 4) he recognizes his role as a caretaker and cultivator of others; 5) he acknowledges his responsibility to be a protector; he is not ready for a serious relationship with a woman nor is he ready to start a family. However, when a man can satisfy these five essential requirements, it is at this time when God will say, "It is not good for the man to be alone" (Genesis 2:18). Otherwise, it is indeed better for the man to remain by himself. All men and women contemplating marriage should heed this advice. It will save you from unspeakable mistakes and will help you avoid unnecessary heartache and pain.

There are times when you have to secure your own needs before you can effectively look after the needs of another. On the surface, this behavior may seem self-centered but there are long-term benefits that warrant such a practice.

12

It's Not About You

Life takes a bit of time and a lot of relationship. – William Paul Young, *The Shack*

No matter how much you love someone, you still want to have your own way. – Chuck Palahniuk, *Lullaby*

When you stop expecting people to be perfect, you can like them for who they are. – Donald Miller

It's not about you. This was the first sentence in the highly successful book The Purpose Driven Life written by Pastor Rick Warren. These words are extremely profound in that it makes it very clear that life is not solely about you. You cannot be completely self-centered if you desire to live a moral life. The feelings, emotions, ideas, aspirations, and opinions of others actually matter and must be taken into consideration in order to foster more meaningful, deeper relationships with other human beings.

Needless to say, there are times when it's appropriate to have a degree of self-centeredness – when you must look after your own well-being and interest. It is vitally important that you take personal responsibility for your mental, physical, and spiritual health, and even your happiness; however, a totally self-centered life will eventually alienate you from developing close relationships with others, which is extremely important. It doesn't matter how much money you have, or how successful you become in your career or in doing business. A life without relationships is a failed life. If you have enough money, you can surround yourself with artificial friends and fake relationships, but someday you will recognize that you don't have anyone special to really talk to or enjoy life with. You will not have an inner circle of people that are close to you, only people who will love you from afar or for what you can do for them.

WHY RELATIONSHIPS ARE IMPORTANT

Love is an intense feeling of deep affection and one of the strongest emotions we can experience. There are many things on earth that we can grow to love. The focus of our love does not have to be on something tangible in order for love to exist. For example, a person can love running, riding a bicycle, singing, eating, or engaging in a myriad of physical activities. Love can also be present for tangible items. We can love money, shoes, handbags, sports cars, etc. However, the true test of whether love is present is best exemplified by our relationship with other humans, as well as our pets.

In order to show love, your affection must be directed at something that can receive and interpret your love. In order for a relationship to flourish and grow, love must also be reciprocated. It's impossible to show love without relationships. Even God could not reveal his nature and true character without relationships. Human beings were created as a manifestation of God's love – so that God could be God, a God of love and relationships. In 1 John 4:8, the beloved apostle says, "But anyone who does not love does not know God, for God *is* love."

Our Creator did not create any living creature with the intent for it to live alone. The survival of the species is dependent upon interactions with others of its kind. Genesis 1:24 makes this clear. Then God said, "Let the earth produce every sort of animal, each producing offspring of the same kind

– livestock, small animals that scurry along the ground and wild animals."

God made all kinds of animals, each able to produce offspring of the same kind. And God saw that it was good. After God created animals, our Creator could now focus his attention on his greatest creation – Man and Woman.

Then God said,

"Let us make human beings in our image, to be like us."…So God created human beings in his own image. In the image of God he created them; male and female he created them (Genesis 1:26-27).

We are not supposed to live our lives alone in solitude. Therefore, it's essential that we interact with other human beings – that we touch, embrace, speak, and hear other human voices. There are consequences if we don't. It has been discovered that babies will literally stop growing if they are not held and hugged enough, even if they are receiving proper nutrition. Sadly, it has been reported that babies raised in orphanages often begin to fear touch unless they begin to receive loving contact from one or two people. Without this, they will not learn how to bond and build relationships, which can spell trouble later in life. The foundation for sustainable, healthy interaction with another human being is built on love.

RESTORING RELATIONSHIPS

Human beings are not perfect. We are flawed in several ways. The apostle Paul said, "Everyone has sinned; we all fall short of God's glorious standard" (Romans 3:23). If we are honest, most of us have annoying idiosyncrasies or extremely bad habits that interfere with maintaining good relationships with others. Often times, two well-meaning people that love each other have difficulty sustaining a long-term relationship and it often results in separation, and all too often divorce.

A friend of mine once told me that divorce is the closest thing to death. Although the person is not dead, it certainly feels like they are because the relationship you once had with them is gone. The feelings, emotions, heartache, and pain that comes with getting a divorce is not easy to overcome. Not only can a divorce negatively affect your attitude, disposition, and outlook on life, it can also adversely affect your children, relatives, and close friends. There are no winners in a divorce.

Couples with children that have divorced, in the best interest of the kids, should find a way to put aside their differences to maintain a cordial relationship. In only the rarest circumstances should a child ever be denied access to their mom or dad. In a way, because of the children created by the union, the father and mother will forever be linked by the combined DNA in their children, long after the divorce is finalized.

Divorce was never supposed to occur. Our Creator did not authorize, sanction, or approve of divorce. Jesus expressed this sentiment to his disciples when he said, "Let no one split apart what God has joined together" (Matthew 19:6). It was expected that the couple would work together to resolve their differences. Unfortunately, because of our inherent weaknesses and personal failures, this is not always the outcome. Jesus would further tell his disciples, "Moses permitted divorce only as a concession to your hard hearts, but it was not what God originally intended" (Matthew 19:8). Even though Jesus stated that divorce is permitted in situations where a spouse has been unfaithful, the hope is that the offending spouse will be forgiven and for the relationship to not end in divorce.

The Book of Hosea is an example of how challenging some marital relationships can be, but it also serves as an example to what extent we should aspire to love, forgive, and restore broken relationships. It reminds us that the Bible is more than a mere collection of theoretical statements with no application to real life. No, it brings to light real issues that work their way into our day-to-day life, while showing the impact of our actions and how it affects relationships.

In the Book of Hosea, the prophet identifies the timeline of his ministry as the middle to late eighth century BC (755-715 BC) by naming the kings that ruled the southern kingdom of Judah and the northern kingdom of Israel. We know very little about Hosea's background, though his book does offer some rather salacious details about his life. Following God's command, Hosea marries a prostitute named Gomer. Over the course of their marriage, Gomer makes a cuckold of him by having multiple affairs and giving birth to two children, a girl and a boy, that he did not father. In the end, despite her unfaithfulness, infidelity, absence, and the considerable amount of embarrassment she caused him, Hosea purchases Gomer's freedom and restores her as his wife.

Hosea's marriage to Gomer is a powerful symbol of redemption and restoration. It's also a profound example of how much God wants us to forgive, redeem, and restore fractured relationships. While Hosea did the unthinkable, staying married to an adulteress wife that engaged in prostitution, God made an even more radical sacrifice – He sent his Son to die in order to restore the relationship with mankind that was damaged by our infidelity of sin.

I don't endeavor to suggest that you should behave in all circumstances like Hosea to save a relationship. There are, of course, situations and circumstances that are so toxic it makes reconciliation impossible. If someone will not change their abusive behavior, it may not be possible to restore the relationship. You do not have the power to change people. But, you do have something within your control, and that is the power to forgive. Through forgiveness, you can release a lot of negative energy and emotions that can keep you from moving forward and putting the past behind you. You may not be able to fully restore a broken relationship, and; you may not want to, but you can at least restore your peace of mind. At the end of the day, your mental health and emotional state is vitally important and must be maintained at all times.

The central theme in the Hosea story, and the entire Bible when you really think about it, is that God values relationships and expects us to make an honest effort to restore damaged relationships, if possible. There are occasions, such as in the story of Hosea, when you have to be the bigger person, taking the first step even when you are not the person at fault. God did the same for you; therefore, you should try to follow His example.

YOU CANNOT BE SUCCESSFUL BY YOURSELF

Nature teaches us that many things have a symbiotic relationship. There are fruit trees that will never bear fruit unless they are pollinated by another tree. The lesson to learn from this is that you cannot be fruitful by yourself. This is true in business and in your personal life. You may regard yourself as the largest contributor and most central figure in your success and achievement, but if you are honest, there are people that were instrumental in helping you get where you are today.

Most likely, a small team of people helped along the way. As the saying goes, there is no "I" in the word team. A quarterback is generally the most important player on a football team, but in order for the team to score a touchdown, many people must do their job properly. A quarterback needs a center that can snap him the football correctly, a running back that will not fumble after being handed the ball, and a receiver that can catch passes thrown their way.

In the business world, any level of success achieved by a company requires a team effort. Chief Executive Officers, the most senior corporate officer, executive, or administrator in charge of managing an organization, because they set the business strategy, often receive too much credit for a company's success. In order to achieve their business strategy, they must have loyal employees that can effectively carry out their plans. If the senior officers in charge of the company's various departments are incompetent and fail to meet each of the given key performance indicators, the organization will not meet all of its strategic objectives.

You are no better than the people around you and the relationships you form.

CHOOSE YOUR FRIENDS AND COMPANIONS CAREFULLY

There is an old saying that you can judge a man by the company he keeps. If this is true, then it's vitally important that you keep good company by surrounding yourself with good people. You should exercise caution in choosing your friends and companions. Not everyone you meet is genuine. Some people are quite good at hiding their true intentions.

When I lived in the Washington, DC metro area, a friend of mine once told me,

"The funny thing about people in this area is that they typically have a hidden motive for wanting to associate with you. They want something from you, and what they want will not be easy to identify. One day, probably several months into your friendship, you will have an epiphany and finally realize their true intent. But by then, they will already have gotten what they want from you. Perhaps you work for a company they have been trying to get an interview with and believe you could be instrumental in making a connection with someone that can influence the hiring decision. Maybe you have a similar interest in clothes and the place where you shop you are able to get good discounts because your best friend is the store manager and alerts you when the store is having a sale. Sometimes it can be something really silly, something as simple as hanging out with you in public because it makes them appear taller or more attractive."

I didn't quite grasp the depth of what my friend said. Unfortunately, I had to learn the profundity of what he said the hard way.

I once dated a woman that seemed to have many things going in her favor. She was very attractive, well educated, had a high paying job, was generally fun to be around, and did not have any children from a prior relationship. To many people's surprise, she was also a good cook. Beauty, brains, a high paying job, and a good cook – you're probably wondering why this woman was still single. Well, no one is perfect. Among a host of other issues, she had a habit of being fashionably late for everything and this included paying her bills on time. Her credit score suffered from this causing a denial of her credit application when she applied for a mortgage loan.

At the time, real estate was booming in many cities across the United States and everyone was trying to get a piece of the action by investing in rental houses and multifamily units. My girlfriend was no different and had high ambitions, but her bad credit prevented her from purchasing something for herself. She needed an investment partner that shared her dream. No one was credulous enough to become an investment partner with her until I came along. Although my salary was considerably less than hers, I had good credit and could get access to bank financing, something she had little hope of obtaining, especially for more expensive properties. After numerous, relentless conversations about becoming an investment partner, she was able to convince me to use my good credit to take out a loan on a four-unit apartment building and include her name on the deed. She would provide the down payment and pay for all expenses including closing costs. The plan was for her to live in one of the units and manage the property. All I had to do was sign my name to the loan documents. In return, she would do the same for me when I had enough money saved to buy a house. She was really convincing and it seemed the right thing to do. I was naïve. I trusted her and fully believed she would honor our agreement.

I was adequately warned not to pursue this course of action by those who were knowledgeable of our proposed arrangement. An attorney friend of mine advised me to formalize our arrangement with a legal contract. Another friend warned me against such action by pointing to scripture that spoke against co-signing loans for others. In concluding his comments, he stated, "If they can't get the property on their own, then they are not supposed to have it." Regrettably, I did not heed their sound advice and purchased the property with her anyway.

As you have probably guessed, things did not go as planned. She reneged on financing a home in my behalf. A few months later, we ended our relationship. A few months after that, I got a better job in another city and relocated. For a little while, she continued to make the payments on the apartment building but eventually fell behind becoming more than 90 days past due. Not long afterward, the bank foreclosed on the property. She lost her investment and I had a foreclosure on my credit history.

I learned many things from this bad experience.

LESSON #1

The first lesson I learned is that you must be mindful of hidden agendas. Not everyone wants to be your friend just because you seem like a nice person. People will often attempt to disguise their true intent, but they will usually say something, if discerned, that will uncover their deception. Upon reflection, I remember that one of the first questions she asked me was whether I had good credit.

LESSON #2

The second lesson is good intentions do not mitigate the harmful consequences that come from ignoring sound advice. It doesn't matter that your heart is in the right place; there are consequences for disobedience. In my case, I disobeyed a biblical command by becoming surety for another person's debt.

The writer of Proverbs felt so strongly about guaranteeing another person's debt that he warned against making this pledge in four different verses (Proverbs 6:1-5, 11:15, 17:18, and 22:26). The Bible is clear on this point, without exception. Never become surety for a friend or anyone outside of your immediate family. If they cannot secure whatever it is they seek on their own, they are not supposed to have it, at least not at that moment, and it's not your responsibility to help them obtain it by putting your financial well-being at risk. You are not morally obligated to help them.

LESSON #3

The third lesson is very simple, "The wicked borrow and never repay" (Psalms 37:21). A person's loan repayment history should alert you to the type of person they are – whether they are honest, responsible, timely, or whether they are dishonest, irresponsible, and perpetually late. Indeed, the world has no shortage of people that constantly search for ways to get something for nothing at the expense of those that work hard, are honest, and will keep their word. Having stated this, I certainly realize that there are unintended life events such as divorce, a death in the family, job loss, and health issues that can lead to financial insolvency, bad credit, and bankruptcy. If such an event occurs, causing someone to fall behind on payments, it does not make them a bad person or a deadbeat. These are extenuating circumstances. However, if you encounter someone that has not experienced any of these aforementioned setbacks, yet they have a track record of not paying their financial obligations on time, you should steer clear of them.

I once had a neighbor who received a NINJA loan to buy a home. A NINJA loan is a slang term for a loan extended to a borrower with "no income, no job, and no assets." These loans were popular before the 2008 financial crisis. My NINJA loan neighbor made a few mortgage payments on their house and then stopped. When foreclosure proceedings commenced, they used legal loopholes to stall the legal process for two and a half years. They rationalized that the bank was wrong for extending them the loan in the first place because the loan officer should have known that they did not have the means to make extended payments. Oddly enough, although all the other homeowners in the community had to go to work each day to be able to make their monthly mortgage payment, this realization somehow escaped them. They honestly believed they were entitled to have a house for free. They assumed the courts would eventually rule in their favor and grant them the house free and clear of a mortgage. Of course, this did not happen and they were eventually evicted. A year later, when one of their children was ready to start college, because of their bad credit, they asked my wife if we would co-sign on their child's student loan. We said no, with the added instruction that it would be irresponsible to guaranty student loan debt for children that are not our own, especially when our oldest child is only a few years away from starting college. They understood. Deep down, they knew their request was entirely unreasonable.

Lesson #4

This brings me to the fourth lesson – givers must put a limit on how much they will give because takers will not put a limit on how much they will attempt to take. Some people are incapable of thinking about anyone other than themselves, pushing the limits of selfish behavior beyond any rational bounds. If you let them, they will feed on you like a vampire that returns each night until you have nothing more to give. Once they have taken everything you have, they will search for their next hapless victim. You have to stop people like this in their tracts by making it clear that there are limits on what you can give and how much you are willing to do. You have to set clear boundaries and define early on the type of relationship you have with them, based on careful observation.

In relationships, people typically assume one of three roles, which are summarized in a book written by Willard F. Harley, Jr. called *Buyers, Renters & Freeloaders: Turning Revolving-Door Romance into Lasting Love*. Buyers, renters, and freeloaders have varying levels of commitment, involvement, and motive. A buyer is someone that will make a considerable investment of time, resources, finances, and emotional involvement to enhance the quality of the relationship. They have a long-term commitment. They will not quickly walk away if problems occur. A renter, unlike a buyer, makes only a marginal investment putting in just enough effort to maintain the status quo. They will continue doing what is required of them as long as they feel that their needs are being met and they are receiving something of equal or greater value in return. A renter is not as committed as a buyer. The moment problems arise that require a greater investment of energy, effort, and time, and if these issues seem too difficult to fix, the renter packs up and leaves. A freeloader is obviously the least favorable of the three persons. A freeloader is not interested in investing anything to enhance the relationship. They are interested only in what they can take or get without any reciprocity. They have zero commitment and will walk away without hesitation the moment you ask for something in return.

I do not encourage you to invest any amount of time in renters and freeloaders if you have a buyer mentality. There is no upside to your involvement. Only invest in building relationships with people that have a "buyer" mentality.

PAY IT FORWARD

Pay It Forward was an American film released in October 2000 based on a novel of the same name by Catherine Ryan Hyde. The plot centered around a seventh-grade class assignment to devise, but more importantly, put into action a plan that would change the world for the better. A 12-year old boy named Trevor McKinney decides to start a charitable program based on the networking of good deeds, a plan he called "pay it forward." The program required a person to perform a favor for a recipient, which had to be something that the recipient could not complete themselves. The recipient then had to perform a favor for three other people rather than paying back the favor. If everyone did this, the act of performing a good deed would go viral and eventually everyone in the world would benefit in some way from random acts of kindness. One notable action in the movie was when Trevor offered shelter to a homeless man who reciprocated the favor by doing car repairs but paid his debt forward in a major way by convincing a suicidal woman from jumping from a bridge.

The act of paying it forward is not a new concept. Often called the golden rule, paying it forward is the essence of Christianity and the foundation on which basic morality is built. Jesus stated the same when he said, "Do to others whatever you would like them to do to you. This is the essence of all that is taught in the law and the prophets" (Matthew 7:12).

The act of performing good deeds should not be an orchestrated performance, such as when a company spokesperson or some rich person announces to the media that they are donating $1 million to charity. Kind acts should not be biased, prejudiced, or based on what you can get in return. Kindness should be spontaneous – done without premeditation;

180

random – not consciously choosing whom the recipient of your action will be, and; timely – occurring at the point when it's most needed. Jesus combines the three – spontaneous, random, and timely, when he tells the Parable of the Good Samaritan found in Luke 10:30-37.

In the story, a Jewish man is attacked by robbers, is severely beaten, stripped of his clothes, and left bloodied and wounded on the side of the road. Three people pass by and see him lying there. The first to pass by was a priest, but upon seeing him moves to the other side of the road to avoid getting too close. The second was a temple assistant, but he acts in a similar manner as the priest. The third person that passed was a Samaritan. Samaritans were regarded as idolatrous and non-Jewish; therefore, Jews were taught not to have any contact with them. Instead of behaving like the priest and temple assistant, the Samaritan approaches the man, soothes his wounds with oil and bandages them, puts him on his donkey, takes him to someone that can take care of him until he is well, and pays for his medical care. The Samaritan had the least to gain from helping the wounded man but showed the most mercy and kindness. His actions were spontaneous, random, and timely. He acted immediately when he saw the man in need, he did not consider whether this man held prejudices against Samaritans, and his act was timely because it occurred when it was needed.

Whenever you help someone, without exception and with no expectation of reciprocity, you are engaging in the highest manifestation of kindness, love, and morality. The size of the act is insignificant. Kind acts do not have to be big in order for them to be relevant. Even small acts of kindness, like holding the door open for someone holding bags, are important. When everyone behaves in a thoughtful manner, stepping outside of their self-centeredness, our cumulative acts of kindness add up to make a meaningful difference and serve to make the world a better place.

Don't wait for someone to help you before you decide to help someone in need. Take the initiative. Over time, you will develop a habit of helping others and this will become part of your character profile.

Chapter Summary

Life is not solely about you – your needs, your wants, and your desires. Besides those in your immediate family and inner circle, apart from friends, co-workers, classmates, and acquaintances, you live on a planet with over 7 billion people, and if you are to get along with others, you have to be mindful of other people's needs and desires. If you decide to take a totally self-centered posture, in due course of time you will find many of your relationships will have become strained and others damaged beyond repair, and contrary to a pervasively wrong opinion, no one has ever become successful without the help of someone else at some point along the way.

Since relationships are vitally important and are a necessary part of life, it's essential that you choose your companions carefully. Be very mindful of those you allow into your inner circle, being careful to acknowledge the tiny clues that may indicate ulterior motives. It's unfortunate, but not everyone wants to be associated with you just because you seem like a nice person. There are people out there that are constantly on the lookout for someone to exploit. Associate with other like-minded people, those that have a buyer's mentality and see the value of investing in people and relationships. Have little contact with people that are renters or freeloaders.

Lastly, pay it forward. Always be ready to help someone that needs assistance. It's simply the right thing to do and it is putting the golden rule, which says to do to others what you would want them to do to you, into practice. A habit of performing kind acts that are spontaneous, random, and timely actually does make a difference in making our world a better place. No matter how small or insignificant your kind acts may seem, they will not go unnoticed.

13

SECURE THEIR FUTURE

The best preparation for the future, is the present well seen to, and the last duty done.
– George MacDonald

Time spent dwelling on the past will surely continue in your present moment – and the future. – Michelle Cruz-Rosado

Have high hopes for the future; take action and it will be a reality. – Debasish Mridha

There was a funny story I read about a stingy old man that loved money so much he wanted to take it with him when he died instead of leaving it to his wife. The story went something like this.

There was a man who had worked all of his life and saved all of his money. He was a real cheapskate when it came to his money. He loved money more than just about anything, and just before he died, he said to his wife..."Now listen, when I die I want you to take all my money and place it in the casket with me. Because I want to take all my money to the afterlife." So he got his wife to promise him with all her heart that when he died...she would put all the money in the casket with him. One day he died. He was stretched out in the casket; the wife was sitting there in black next to their best friend. When they finished the ceremony, just before the undertakers got ready to close the casket, the wife said, "Wait a minute!" She had a shoebox with her; she came over with the box and placed it in the casket. Then the undertakers locked the casket and rolled it away. Her friend said, "I hope you weren't crazy enough to put all that money in there with that stingy old man." She said, "Yes, I promised. I'm a good Christian, I can't lie. I promised him that I was to put that money in that casket with him." 'You mean to tell me you put every cent of his money in that box.' She said, "Of course I did. I wrote him a check."

The way the man's wife circumvented his request was ingenious. The satire is meant to make you laugh. However, in reality, people die each day and leave their spouse and children with nothing but memories, and there is nothing funny about this. Unlike the stingy old man in the story, they do not die and leave their family without money on purpose, but the outcome is the same. Not only must their spouse and children deal with the pain of losing a loved one, they must sometimes grapple with the hardship of losing a source of income.

LIFE INSURANCE

Even in advanced countries, there are millions of people living without life insurance. The thought of dying is something the average person does not contemplate each day. Therefore, death is not something that one prepares for. This is irresponsible, especially if you have dependents. The difficulty of death is compounded tenfold if the person is not independently wealthy and dies without life insurance. We all have an expiry date so the reality of death is nothing that should take us by surprise. However, dying without life insurance and leaving your family with nothing is a tragedy that can, and should, be avoided.

Several times, I have personally observed the unintended consequences and hardship that is caused when someone dies without life insurance. I have had friends directly ask me for money and been in church services where a collection is taken up to help defray the costs of a funeral. While needing assistance to bury a loved one may be embarrassing, it's not tragic. What is tragic is dying without life insurance when you have a family to support, particularly when you are the primary breadwinner or the only source of income.

Your family should not have to ask for assistance or borrow money from others to cover your burial. At a minimum, you should have sufficient life insurance to cover the costs of the funeral service and burial procedures. Additional life insurance coverage is needed if there are outstanding debts that others have cosigned and are legally required to pay. If you have underage dependents, the amount of life insurance needed increases exponentially. The rule of thumb offered by financial advisors is life insurance coverage should be ten times your annual salary. For example, if the spouse earns $30,000 a year they should have a life insurance policy of $300,000. Following this advice should leave the family with enough money to pay off debts, secure housing, and provide the children with funds for future education expenses. It will not ensure the remaining spouse a life free from work, but it does leave them with a solid foundation to build upon – they will not have to worry about accommodation costs or hide from debt collectors.

You should do your level best to leave your spouse and dependents with more than just your good name. A simple term life insurance policy is affordable if you are in reasonably good health. When you consider that the monthly premium payment of a life insurance policy is cheaper than the average cell phone bill, there is no excuse for not having a policy.

Leave A Legacy

Proverbs 13:22 says a good person leaves an inheritance for their children's children. Few things are more valuable than a thriving family business. A family business is a storehouse of

187

accumulated wealth that can be passed down to preserve wealth for future generations. Leaving your heirs with a thriving business should be the endeavor of every parent.

In chapter 9, you read about the numerous benefits and reasons why you should start your own business. Aside from the independence and wealth it creates, owning a business allows you to leave a legacy for your children. A business is something they can reap benefits from before you depart this earth. If children are given the opportunity, or made, to participate in the family business when they are young, they can learn responsibility, hard work, problem-solving, communication skills, time management, thrift, finance, and economics sooner – vital skills that are necessary in life.

Another reason why a family business is important is that it can eliminate the uncertainty of your children obtaining a good job. There are too many underemployed young adults still living at home with their parents because they could not find suitable employment. If you own your own business, you have the power to hire your children without anyone questioning your authority. Contrast this with working for a company. Very few senior managers are empowered to create jobs for their children. There are checks and balances that prevent nepotism. Even if you consider yourself an owner of a company because you possess a few hundred shares of stock, if you do not have the power to give your children a job you are not an owner! They must still go with their résumé in hand to job fairs in hope of finding a job. Frankly, I want to save my children from this experience, if only to prevent reducing their qualifications, education, and life experience to a few lines of text and bullet points on a fancy sheet of paper called a résumé.

Your children may not want to work in the family business long-term, particularly if it requires physical labor or getting dirty. When they become adults, they will have to charter their own course in life by making their own decisions. If they decide to venture out on their own and work for another company or business, they may later decide, like the parable of the prodigal son found in Luke 15, it's a tough world out there and life is better at home. By owning your own business, at least you will be empowered to help them in a time of need and give them options.

If you are not in a position to leave your children an inheritance, it's not the end of the world. With children, it's not how much you leave them that makes them great; it's how much you leave inside them. If you leave more to them than what you leave inside of them, they may squander everything you left them. However, if you leave more inside of them than what you left them, then you do not have to leave as much to them because they can go out and make their own way in life. As their parent, one of your responsibilities is to teach them and create opportunities so that they can have more options to secure the future they desire.

CHAPTER SUMMARY

You enter this world naked, and you will take nothing with you when you die. That doesn't mean that you should leave your loved ones with nothing when you depart. The Bible says a good man leaves an inheritance for their children's children. Your children did not seek permission from you to be born. They did not have a choice. Therefore, you should be mindful to secure their welfare until the time comes when they are able to provide for themselves.

One of the best things you can leave your family is a well-managed and financially sound business. This will ensure their future and can provide wealth for future generations. If you do not have a legacy to leave behind, be sensible enough to ensure that you have a life insurance policy and are adequately covered. A rule of thumb is ten times your annual income. At a minimum, make sure the coverage is sufficient to cover the costs of your funeral.

PART 4

TRAITS THAT LEAD TO SUCCESS

It is through strength of character, not luck, do we form the predictable path of our future. – Shannon L. Alder

Never give up. This applies to more than goals and dreams, it is a maximum for basic daily struggles. It shapes one's life, including the will to continue to live. It supports love and committed relationships; it bolsters hope, faith, and charity; it is power in every area of existence. Never give up on anything of any worth, especially yourself. – Richelle E. Goodrich

Allow yourself to think only those thoughts that match your principles and can bear the bright light of day. Day by day, your choices, your thoughts, your actions fashion the person you become. Your integrity determines your destiny. – Heraclitus

14

Traits That God Admires

Character is doing what you don't want to do but know you should do. – Joyce Meyer

A man is literally what he thinks, his character being the complete sum of all his thoughts. – James Allen, *As A Man Thinketh*

Talent is a gift, but character is a choice. – John C. Maxwell

No matter what part of the world you're from, there are common human traits and characteristics we share that are admired. In a soldier, we admire courage. In an athlete, we admire competitiveness. In a teacher, we admire commitment. In a political leader, we admire integrity.

Your character traits are what define you and can sometimes define an entire nation. For example, Chinese and Indian students that come to the United States are well known for their work ethic and fortitude in pursuing the more difficult science and math classes in school. Americans are known for their hope and belief that there can be a better tomorrow. The message of hope became a theme during Barack Obama's first campaign for president and was expressed in the slogan "Yes we can."

There are human qualities and traits embedded in the character of man that embody the brilliance and magnificence of our being. I believe that God admires certain traits in mankind – some traits more than others.

My favorite person and chronicle in the Bible is the story of Joseph – the boy with the coat of many colors, the son of Jacob, grandson of Isaac, and great-grandson of Abraham. The story and life of Joseph appears in Genesis chapters 37, 39 – 50.

I enjoy the life and story of Joseph for several reasons. It's an amazing story that shows the twists, the turns, and the difficulties of life. It shows the best and worst in human behavior.

Joseph's life is a mixture of the *Count of Monte Cristo* and the Nelson Mandela experience rolled into one. Most importantly, I believe that the story and life of Joseph reveals a few of the most desirable character traits found in mankind, and these traits will set you up for future success. Very shortly, you will discover what I believe are the most outstanding character traits that God admires. First, let me provide a brief reminder, and for others a new awareness, of the life of Joseph.

Joseph was one of twelve sons. He was the second youngest son and the one his father, Jacob, loved the most.

Jacob had children by four different women; two were wives and two were concubines. The two wives were sisters. Their names were Leah and Rachel. Leah was the older of the two sisters. The other two women were Jacob's concubines – handmaids for Leah and Rachel.

Jacob's father-in-law and uncle, Laban, told Jacob that he would allow him to marry his youngest daughter, Rachel, if he would work for him. However, Laban tricked Jacob and gave him Leah to marry instead. Jacob was allowed to marry Rachel too, but this would be the cause, and the beginning, of a great deal of conflict in Jacob's home.

Leah very quickly gave Jacob six sons – seven children in total. Rachel struggled to get pregnant and – not wanting to be outdone by her sister – encouraged Jacob to sleep with her handmaid, Bilhah, so that she might have children through her. Bilhah gave Jacob two sons. Leah, not wanting to be overshadowed by her sister, encouraged Jacob to sleep with her handmaid, Zilpah, as well. Zilphah gave Jacob two sons. It was not until much later when Rachel was able to conceive. She gave birth to Joseph and Benjamin, the youngest of the twelve brothers. Unfortunately, Rachel died shortly after giving birth to Benjamin.

Trait #1 - Impartiality

This was not a model family.

A monogamous marriage has its challenges. Imagine what it's like having four women competing for the attention of one man at the same time. This household had jealousy, bickering, arguing, fighting, to name just a few things. Name any type of internal discord and it was probably evident in this household. It was like watching an episode of ABC's *The Bachelor*. What made matters worse was that children were involved.

Jacob had many flaws. He was certainly not the model husband and was not the model father. Jacob showed favoritism in relationships – he openly favored one of his wives and one of his sons more than he did the others.

Jacob loved Joseph, Rachel's oldest son, more than his other sons. To show his love and affection, Jacob gave Joseph a coat with many colors; it was a very expensive and elaborate gift.

Joseph's brothers became jealous and hated him for the favoritism he was shown. Joseph, unfortunately, made matters worse for himself by revealing two dreams to his brothers and father that he should have probably kept private.

> "He said unto them, 'Listen to this dream I had: we were binding sheaves of grain out in the field when suddenly my sheaf rose and stood upright, while your sheaves gathered around mine and bowed down to it'...then he had another dream, and he told it to his brothers. 'I had another dream, and this time the sun and the moon and eleven stars were bowing down to me'" (Genesis 37:6-7, 9).

Imagine your little brother, on two separate occasions, telling you that he has dreamed about you and all your brothers bowing down to him – and this comes after your father has openly favored him all of his life.

Telling his brothers about his dream was not very smart. In fact, it was a rather boastful and annoying act and this caused his brothers to voice their disdain (Genesis 37:8). Jacob also rebuked his son (Genesis 37:10).

If telling his brothers his dreams were meant as a joke, it wasn't very funny.

Before I go any further, allow me to make some rather important points. Although Joseph did not exercise the best judgment by sharing his dream with his brothers, it shows that he was not afraid to dream big. Joseph knew that he was special – and perhaps one day all his brothers would really bow down to him, including his father. In spite of his father's rebuke, the Bible doesn't suggest Joseph ever wavered from his belief or challenged the idea that what he dreamed was just a dream and had no real-life application. Even Jacob wondered about the credibility of his son's dream. But little did he know at the time just how powerful his son, Joseph, would become.

I need to make another important point clear. Your thoughts and dreams are a compass that guides your achievement. Small dreams create low achievement. Big dreams create high achievement.

The story of Joseph gets even more interesting.

Jacob sends Joseph to check on his ten older brothers who have gone out to feed their father's flocks. When Joseph draws near to them, wearing his coat of many colors, they conspire and plot to kill him. The plan is to murder Joseph and tell their father that a wild animal has devoured him. The only brother that did not want to see Joseph dead was Rueben, the eldest son. Imagine your siblings hating you so much that almost all of them want to see you dead.

If you have children, showing favoritism is destructive. No child should ever feel inferior or not as important and loved as another.

Jacob's manner of expressing love was misguided and wrong. Because he was tricked into marrying Leah, when Rachel was the woman he truly loved, Jacob gave his wives unequal love and affection. The scripture is clear that Leah did not feel equally loved. Leah gave Jacob six sons. It's a reasonable assumption that Jacob didn't sleep with Leah only six times. The same is probably true for the concubines. Nowhere does the Bible state that Jacob ever refused any of the four women. It doesn't state that Jacob said, "No Leah, I won't sleep with you tonight." Nor does he say, "I'm sorry Rachel. I won't sleep with your handmaid."

Jacob showed outright favoritism and failed to love his wives and children equally.

It's hard to find a more dysfunctional family.

TRAIT #2 - FIDELITY

If someone believes that Jacob was a lucky man, because he could be intimate with four women at the same time, they are wrong. There are consequences for such behavior. Having a monogamous relationship with one woman is not always easy. Trying to manage a relationship with multiple women at the same time is a recipe for grief and misery, especially when children are present. There can be lifelong repercussions. In fact, problems among the children can go on for thousands of years. Abraham, Jacob's grandfather, had Ishmael through a concubine and there has been tension among his children's offspring ever since. Yet there is still hope that the conflict will one day be resolved.

Almost every story in the Bible where a patriarch or king has more than one wife shows some level of dysfunction.

King David's house became divided due to him having multiple children by different women. One of David's sons raped his half-sister. And later, one of his sons, Absalom, tried to seize David's throne by force.

The birth of Samuel is another example of a dysfunctional family because of multiple wives. Samuel's father, Elkanah, had two wives – Hannah and Peninnah. Peninnah had several children, but Hannah had none. Because of her bareness, Hannah cried to the Lord daily so that she might have a son.

Imagine having a wife that cries every day and is so miserable that she cannot eat. To make matters worse, your other wife is helping to provoke her misery by being mean – always reminding her that she cannot give their husband children.

The list of men in the Bible that have multiple wives is incomplete without Solomon. The Bible reports that Solomon had 700 wives and 300 concubines. Can you believe it! When Solomon was old, his multiple wives led him to worship idols and other gods besides Jehovah.

Too much of anything can lead to trouble.

TRAIT #3 - RESOLVE

Now, back to Joseph.

Rueben didn't want his brothers to kill Joseph so he recommended that they throw him into a pit instead. It was Rueben's plan to remove Joseph from the pit and return him to their father. However, before he could rescue Joseph from the pit, his brothers sold him to merchants that were passing by traveling to Egypt. These merchants were actually distant cousins. They were Ishmaelites, descendants of Ishmael, the first-born son of Abraham, the father of the Muslims. The Midianite merchants sold Joseph as a slave in Egypt to an officer of Pharaoh, who was a captain of the palace guard.

Imagine the fear this young man must have felt. All he had previously known was the comfort of his father's home. Now he is without family, friends, and is a slave in a distant land. He is totally alone. It's fair to assume that he didn't even speak the language!

Not many people could survive being sold into slavery. In fact, many people would probably lose all hope. Some might even commit suicide. Not Joseph. He did the opposite of what you would expect.

Joseph did not allow his circumstance to paralyze him with fear and snatch away his hope. He decided to make the best of a very challenging situation. He was not going to allow the fact that he was a slave beat him into submission and cause him to give up on life. If life gave him lemons, he would make lemonade.

Joseph did everything he was asked to do, and then did more. He exceeded expectations. He was the type of person who arrived early to work and then stayed late. It didn't matter that he was only paid minimum wage (actually, Joseph was a slave so he did not receive a wage). He gave 100%. He epitomized the meaning of the phrase "safe hands." If you asked Joseph to do something, you could rest assured that it would be done correctly and timely – no matter the task. Joseph was the blueprint for the model employee.

Few people have Joseph's determination to exceed standards, especially when they feel their hard work is not rewarded – when they fail to be promoted or receive a raise. Many people proudly boast that if you pay them minimum wage, you are going to get a minimum effort in return. Perhaps that's where the phrase "you get what you pay for" comes from.

Joseph didn't have this mindset.

God noticed.

Genesis 39:2-3 says, "The Lord was with Joseph so that he prospered...and that the Lord gave him success in everything he did."

Don't misunderstand and believe that the Lord prospered Joseph because He felt sorry for him. Joseph's circumstance is not what got the Lord's attention. Joseph wasn't the first slave in Egypt and wasn't the last. Bad things happen to good people all the time.

What made the Lord notice Joseph and prosper him in everything he did?

It was Joseph's character.

God is not impressed with physical attributes. He doesn't regard height, beauty, age, or gender. These things are unimportant to God. The Bible says that people look at the outward appearance, but the Lord looks at the heart (1 Samuel 16:7).

Your physical attributes will eventually deteriorate. However, one quality you have that can get better over time is your character. Your character is what the Lord is more concerned about and wants to see restored. When Adam and Eve sinned, their Godly character was the first of many things that were lost.

Character development is why God sent the prophets. Character is what Jesus looked for when he searched for disciples and is what he found so little of during his ministry on earth.

It was Joseph's character and the strength of his resolve that got the Lord's attention.

When the Lord took inventory of the people on earth, He noticed a young man that had qualities He could use.

Joseph had resolve, and not just a little. Joseph's resolve and determination were so exceptional that the Lord took notice. The Lord knew Joseph's character, but it had to be tested. The Lord allowed Joseph to be sold into slavery. He allowed this poor young man to become frightened, humiliated, discouraged, and stripped of his freedom as a testament to the world of what good character looks like.

The Lord wasn't disappointed. He observed Joseph respond by embracing his situation and determining within himself that he was going to be the best that he could be despite his circumstance.

You may not be aware that you possess a certain character trait until an event in life gives you an opportunity to show it.

Joseph's attitude, combined with the Lord's favor, created an environment that made Joseph's master take notice. The captain of the guard was no fool. He knew exactly what to do.

The Bible records that Joseph found favor in the eyes of his Egyptian master.

> Potiphar put him in charge of his household, and he entrusted to his care everything he owned. From the time he put him in charge of his household and of all that he owned, the Lord blessed the household of the Egyptian because of Joseph. The blessing of the Lord was on everything Potiphar had, both in the house and in the field. So Potiphar left everything he had in Joseph's care; with Joseph in charge, he did not concern himself with anything except the food he ate (Genesis 39:5-6).

God uses individuals with a sound character as examples of how we are to conduct ourselves. It is worth noting that God does not require perfect people, people that have never made a mistake. God is looking for people with strong character.

TRAIT #4 - INTEGRITY

The dictionary defines integrity as *a firm adherence to a code of especially moral or artistic values*. I define integrity as the soundness of mind to do the right thing when: 1) it is easy to do wrong; 2) no one else is looking; 3) when the chance of a wrong act going unpunished is high.

Let's face it. Doing the right thing is not always fun. In fact, life seems to provide more reward and pleasure when you do the wrong things. The more you are told not to do something, the more you want to do it. Many people have felt excited or a rush of adrenaline when engaging in an act they know is wrong or know others will disapprove of. Some say it's the thrill of the possibility that you might get caught that makes the act so exciting.

Joseph had an opportunity to do the wrong thing – when doing the wrong thing was actually encouraged, and when the chance of being caught was slim. However, the situation that Joseph found himself in was not one where many men would have exercised the same restraint and shown a similar level of integrity.

The Bible says that Joseph was very good looking. He was a young man in his early twenties. The wife of his master took notice. Genesis 39:7 says, 'Now Joseph was well-built and handsome, and after a while his master's wife took notice of Joseph and said, "Come to bed with me!"' (Gen 39:7).

Joseph refused, telling her,

"Look, my master trusts me with everything in his entire household. No one here has more authority than I do. He has held back nothing from me except you, because you are his wife. How could I do such a wicked thing? It would be a great sin against God." She kept putting pressure on him day after day, but he refused to sleep with her, and he kept out of her way as much as possible (Gen 39:8-10).

The Bible does not specify how this woman looked or what her age may have been. However, it's highly likely that she was very attractive. It would have been very easy for a man with Potiphar's wealth and position to have his choice of several attractive women in Egypt. Therefore, it's reasonable to assume that the woman Joseph rejected, even if she were older than himself, was a very attractive woman.

Put yourself in Joseph's sandals for just a moment. Imagine going to work every day and your boss's wife, who works there too, keeps asking you to go to bed with her. You are single, in your early twenties, and your hormones are at their peak! Moreover, there seems little chance that you will be caught.

These factors would cause many men to succumb to temptation. Some men would probably question their manhood if they did not accept her advances.

Not Joseph.

His integrity and moral compass were so resilient that when she grabbed him by his clothes and begged him to sleep with her, he pulled himself from her grasp, leaving his garment in her hand, and fled from the house (Genesis 39:12).

Joseph was unwilling to sin against God and commit evil by sleeping with another man's wife. He exercised restraint when it would have been easy to do wrong. No one was looking. There was little chance of him being caught. Joseph's actions epitomized the definition of integrity and provided a real-life example for us to follow.

TRAIT #5 - PERSEVERANCE

Joseph's display of honor, integrity, and veracity did not produce the results that one might expect. The sad truth is that it backfired. Potiphar's wife did not beg for his forgiveness and promise never to approach him in an inappropriate manner again. She did something entirely dishonorable. She accused Joseph of attempted rape.

The Bible says,

> When she saw that she was holding his cloak and he had fled, she called out to her servants. Soon all the men came running. "Look!" she said. "My husband has brought this Hebrew slave here to make fools of us! He came into my room to rape me, but I screamed. When he heard me scream, he ran outside and got away, but he left his cloak behind me." She kept the cloak with her until her husband came home. Then she told him her story. "That Hebrew slave you've brought into our house tried to come in and fool around with me," she said. "But when I screamed, he ran outside, leaving his cloak with me (Gen 39:13-18)!"

When Potiphar heard his wife's story he burned with anger and had Joseph thrown into prison.

For Joseph, things had just gone from bad to worse. It wasn't enough that his brothers unmercifully sold him into slavery. Now, he was wrongfully accused of a crime that he did not commit. Suddenly, with one incriminating lie, everything that he had worked to build, his honor and reputation, was destroyed. He went from being a trusted and respected servant to a vile sex offender.

As a trusted slave in charge of his master's home and affairs, Joseph was allowed a moderate degree of freedom. He could eat good food. He could enjoy the comfort of a decent bed. He could wear clean clothes and take regular baths. He could enjoy the company and conversation of others. Not anymore. Now, his surroundings would be limited to the confines of the prison. Food would be infrequent, of poor quality, and would probably not taste very good. His clothing would be tattered and dirty. The putrid smell of body odor, filth, feces, and urine would be all around him. A clean, hot bath could only be experienced in a dream.

Life can be very unfair. Bad things happen to good people all the time. A person can lose their job due to cost cutting, lose their home to foreclosure, lose their health, and lose a parent or a child in a tragic accident. However, few things compare to being forced to serve prison time for a crime that you didn't commit. It's hard to imagine the grief, anger, and hopelessness that Joseph must have felt.

However, the Bible tells us that Joseph was able to persevere while in prison. He didn't allow his living conditions to change him. Joseph maintained the same work ethic, honor, and integrity that allowed him to prosper in Potiphar's house. His mind was made up. No matter what happened to him, he was going to honor God by not giving in to despondency, bitterness, cursing, apathy, laziness, idolatry, and revengeful sin. Joseph did not allow his spirit to become completely broken and unfit for the Lord to use. Had Joseph given in to all the debilitating and paralyzing feelings that he must have felt, he would have negated his ability to overcome his circumstances. His feelings would have utterly destroyed all fragments of hope to carry him through this trying time.

Hope is defined as *the feeling that what is wanted can be had, or that events will turn out for the best.*

When life becomes difficult, it is very important that you don't give up and lose hope.

You must maintain hope.

You must also not lose faith.

Why?

Paul tells you that, "Without faith it is impossible to please God, because anyone who comes to him must believe that he exists and that he rewards those who earnestly seek him" (Hebrews 11:6). Paul also tells you that, "Faith is confidence in what we hope for and assurance about what we do not see" (Hebrews 11:1).

One of the primary ingredients of hope is faith, and faith is developed by seeing a positive outcome from life experiences and trials. The ability to endure difficult circumstances of unknown duration without complaining is patience. The brother of Jesus informs you to,

> "Consider it pure joy...whenever you face trials of many kinds, because you know that the testing of your faith produces perseverance. Let perseverance finish its work so that you may be mature and complete, not lacking anything" (James 1:2-4).

Paul and James are informing you that challenging life events should be expected. The challenge is not as important as the way you respond. Whenever a test or trial comes your way, the first thing you should realize is that the battle is won by perseverance and enduring to the end. You must have enough faith to believe in a positive outcome. You must have hope that there will be better days. You must be patient and wait for a breakthrough. Finally, you must persevere by maintaining a clear purpose in spite of difficulty, obstacles, and discouragement – no matter what you are going through.

Perseverance is a Godly trait, and God absolutely loves persevering people. God knows that persevering people will endure to the end. Persevering people are not despondent. In the face of adversity, even death, they are optimistic. Their faith, combined with unrelenting patience, keeps burning and will push away the darkness of adversity. A battle-tested persevering man or woman is like a navy seal or an army ranger. You can count on them to complete the task.

Jesus Christ, despite being led like a lamb to slaughter, was able to complete his mission of going to the cross.

God admires people that can keep going when things get tough. He admires individuals who, like Paul, can say, "I have fought the good fight, I have finished the race, I have kept the faith" (2 Tim 4:7).

Joseph's perseverance was rewarded. Because Joseph was diligent in performing his duties while he was in prison – as he was in Potiphar's house – the Lord blessed him. Favor would not have been shown Joseph if he allowed himself to become an indolent prisoner that spent the majority of his time feeling sorry for himself. Because of Joseph's responsible nature and safe hands, the prison warden,

> "put Joseph in charge of all those held in the prison, and he was made responsible for all that was done there. The warden paid no attention to anything under Joseph's care, because the Lord was with Joseph and gave him success in whatever he did" (Genesis 39:22).

Just like with Potiphar, the prison warden trusted Joseph so much that he didn't bother micromanaging him or reviewing his work.

Joseph did not allow his situation to defeat him. Instead, he accepted the lemons that life gave him and made lemonade. He made the best of a bad situation. Because of his attitude and pleasant demeanor, while suffering adversity, the Lord blessed him so that he gained favor in the eyes of the prison warden.

A man or woman who has faith in God, is patient, and is able to persevere through challenging circumstances, and still maintain a Godly character, is a person after God's own heart.

Their actions will not go unnoticed.

Their situation will improve.

They will be rewarded.

TRAIT #6 - HUMILITY

If there are character traits in mankind that God admires, then the opposite must also be true – there are character traits that He hates. One of the traits that God hates is arrogance – exalting yourself or thinking more highly of yourself than you do of others. God feels so strongly about arrogance, it's mentioned first among six hated traits and actions.

"These six things the Lord hates, seven that are detestable to Him: haughty eyes, a lying tongue, hands that shed innocent blood, a heart that devises wicked schemes, feet that are quick to rush to evil, a false witness who pours out lies, and one who stirs up conflict in the community" (Proverbs 6:16-19).

God places arrogance in the same category as liars and murderers.

Haughtiness, also called arrogance, may be allowed to endure for a season, but eventually arrogant thoughts, words, and behavior will cause you to be brought low. If God did not allow an angel to escape punishment for his continued arrogance – and subsequently, the discord that came later – don't expect that you, a human, will be treated differently.

"How you are fallen from heaven, O Lucifer, son of the morning! How you are cut down to the ground – mighty though you were against the nations of the world. For you said to yourself, "I will ascend to heaven and rule the angels. I will take the highest throne. I will preside on the Mount of Assembly far away in the north. I will climb to the highest heavens and be like the Most High. But instead, you will be brought down to the pit of hell, down to its lowest depths" (Isaiah 14:12-15).

The antonym of arrogance is humility. It should be no surprise that if God hates arrogance, He must love humility.

God personified humility through Jesus Christ. No one in earth's history was more humble than Jesus. Jesus, who was with God and who was God (John 1:1), came to earth to live among the poor. He could have come to earth as the son of a king – having power, riches, and honor. Instead, he came and took the form of a commoner. He was poor, accustomed to sorrow, grief,

210

and want. The Bible even tells us that Jesus was not good looking.

> "There was nothing beautiful or majestic about his appearance, nothing to attract us to him. He was rejected – a man of sorrows, acquainted with grief. We turned our backs on him and looked the other way. He was despised, and we did not care" (Isaiah 53:2-3).

Jesus, the only begotten of the Father, whom the angels adore and worship, came to earth to be a servant. He never boasted or exalted himself above others. He served mankind whole-heartedly while knowing that the people he came to serve would kill him. No one is more deserving of our honor, respect, admiration, and love.

Humility is God's character personified. Therefore, whenever people display humility God's nature is revealed.

Humility was evident in Joseph. During Joseph's tenure in prison, two of the king's servants were put in prison and placed under his care. One servant was the king's cupbearer; the other was the king's baker. Both the baker and cupbearer had troubling dreams. When Joseph asked why they looked so sad they told him about their disturbing dreams.

> "We both had dreams last night, but no one can tell us what they mean."

> "Interpreting dreams is God's business," Joseph replied. "Go ahead and tell me your dreams." (Genesis 40:8)

Note Joseph's response very carefully. He did not take credit for being able to provide the interpretation of dreams. He gives God the credit. He acknowledges that he is merely a vessel that God uses to tell the meaning of dreams.

Joseph says a similar statement to Pharaoh before he tells him the meaning of a dream that he recently had, "It is beyond my power to do this. But God can tell you what it means and set you at ease" (Genesis 41:16). With such an honest and humble character, Pharaoh could not resist elevating Joseph to a position of authority. After Joseph interprets Pharaoh' dream, he is released from prison and becomes the second most powerful man in Egypt.

Joseph was confident in his abilities, but he was never arrogant. He was careful to give God the credit, instead of boasting of his own abilities.

TRAIT #7 - DECISIVENESS

Have you ever met someone that is indecisive, who can't make up their mind, and goes back and forth between decisions?

Knowing someone that has trouble making concrete decisions can be frustrating, particularly if it adversely affects you in some way. If you are like me, then you have learned not to make plans with indecisive people. Through experience, I've learned that indecisive people are unreliable. Because they find it hard to make timely, resolute, and concrete decisions, their indecisiveness will inevitably waste valuable time and resources.

Do you know another admirable character trait that Joseph had?

Decisiveness.

God appreciates people that are focused, that know what they want, and have a plan for how they are going to get it.

Even with prayer, God wants to hear meaningful, directed, and well thought out prayer requests. He is reluctant to answer your prayer request if you keep changing your mind. The Bible says, "For let not that man suppose that he will receive anything from the Lord; he is a double-minded man, unstable in all his ways" (James 1:7-8).

God is much more likely to support the ideas, plans, and actions of decisive people who say what they are going to do, then actually do it.

Right after Joseph interprets Pharaoh's dream, he immediately instructs Pharaoh of a plan of action to mitigate the damage of the famine that will occur in seven years.

> "Therefore, Pharaoh should find an intelligent and wise man and put him in charge of the entire land of Egypt. Then Pharaoh should appoint supervisors over the land and let them collect one-fifth of all the crops during the seven good years. Have them gather all the food produced in the good seven years that are just ahead and bring it to Pharaoh's storehouses. Store it away, and guard it so there will be food in the cities" (Genesis 41:33-35).

If you say you are going to do something, do it. Don't spend a lot of time merely talking about it. Get to work and make it happen.

TRAIT #8 - FORGIVENESS

The story of Joseph is not complete without discussing his incredible ability to forgive. In fact, out of all his remarkable character traits, you can easily make an argument that forgiveness was the most amazing.

Just as Joseph predicted, there were seven years of plenty followed by seven years of famine. In fact, the seven-year famine contributed to one of the largest wealth transfers in history! People from all countries came to Egypt to buy grain from Joseph year after year. After the people spent all of their money to buy grain, they would later exchange their livestock for food. Yet the famine still carried on. Finally, with nothing else to give, and their situation remaining desperate, the people said,

> "We cannot hide the truth from you, my Lord. Our money is gone, and all our livestock and cattle are yours. We have nothing left to give but our bodies and our land. Why should we die before your very eyes? Buy us and our land in exchange for food; we offer our land and ourselves as slaves for Pharaoh. Just give us grain so we may live and not die, and so the land does not become empty and desolate" (Genesis 47:18-19).

Joseph's father, his brothers, and their families were also adversely affected by the famine. Like everyone else in the region, they also had to come to Egypt to buy grain.

> When Jacob heard that grain was available in Egypt, he said to his sons, "Why are you standing around looking at one another? I have heard that there is grain in Egypt. Go down there, and buy enough grain to keep us alive. Otherwise we'll die" (Genesis 42:1-2).

Joseph's brothers went to Egypt to buy grain, but his younger brother, Benjamin, did not come during their first trip.

> Since Joseph was governor of all of Egypt and in charge of selling grain to all the people, it was to him that his brothers came. When they arrived, they bowed before him with their faces to the ground. Joseph recognized his brothers

instantly, but he pretended to be a stranger" (Genesis 42:6-7).

The brother's show of respect by kneeling was the fulfillment of Joseph's childhood dream. But, this was not the time for Joseph to say, "I told you so."

Joseph's brothers did not recognize him, and he would not reveal his true identity to them at this time. It was during their second trip to Egypt to buy grain, with Benjamin present, that Joseph would reveal himself to his brothers.

After their character was tested, in a remarkable display of love and forgiveness, Joseph asked his brothers to fetch their father and to bring their families, livestock, and possessions and return to Egypt. He will look after them and ensure their comfort and survival (Genesis 45:9-11, 17) by allowing them to eat from the best the land produces. He embraces and kisses each of them. When he sends them away to retrieve their belongings, Joseph tells them, "Don't quarrel about this along the way!"

Can you imagine a more incredible display of love and forgiveness?

As if this story was not already incredibly awesome, Joseph shows that he is so concerned about his brother's state of mind he tells them not to quarrel with each other along the way, just in case they are still angry with themselves for what they did to him.

Joseph has already forgiven them. Now, he wants them to forgive themselves.

Joseph could have easily treated his brothers harshly, but he didn't. He could have decided not to forgive them and left them to suffer. Few people will fault him.

Imagine. Your brothers sell you into slavery and later appear before you to buy food.

How would you respond?

Like Joseph?

Joseph did not seek revenge. He didn't even lecture them about morality. He simply forgave them. He turned any negative sentiments he had towards them into positive energy. This is an important lesson to learn.

CHAPTER SUMMARY

Everyone is known for something. In the end, your character is what truly defines you – your character is most important. Therefore, it seems rather important to develop specific character traits that matter most – the ones that God admires and will reward in this life and the next.

This chapter discussed eight character traits: impartiality, fidelity, resolve, perseverance, integrity, humility, decisiveness, and forgiveness – that are truly important for personal development and success in life. Joseph, the boy in the Bible that wore a coat of many colors, was an extraordinary human being that possessed all eight traits and was rewarded by God – rising to the second highest position in Egypt after arriving as a slave and spending time in prison.

While you should never lose sight that God is the most important being that you should revere, you can also strive to model the life and develop the best personality traits seen in

Godly people. After Jesus, if you want someone to emulate, look no further than Joseph.

About the Author

Terrence is also the author of *The Tithing Conspiracy: Exposing the Lies & False Teachings About Tithing and the Prosperity Gospel*. Terrence was employed as a COBOL programmer, research associate, pricing analyst, and a bank regulator for Central Banks. In addition to writing, he is passionate about empowering people to live a fuller life through education and pursuing their dreams to achieve financial freedom. He is also passionate about investing in organic mini-farm operations to achieve food security and to end domestic hunger. The revenue earned from this book will go towards investing in these pursuits.

You can find out more about Terrence by going to his website at www.TerrenceJameson.com. Visit the website to join the email list so you can be notified of future book releases and promotions.

Made in the USA
Las Vegas, NV
29 January 2022

42555427R00125